Gemstone Buying Guide

How to evaluate, identify select and care for colored gems

Second Edition

Custom rubellite necklace and bracelet accented with diamonds. Both were hand-fabricated by Hubert Inc., and the rubellites were cut by Itamar Pimenta at Hubert Inc. *Photo by Harold & Erica Van Pelt.*

Opposite page: An array of aquamarine, green grossular garnet, yellow sapphire, blue sapphire, pink spinel and lavender spinel from the Cynthia Renée, Company. *Photo by Robert Weldon.*

Gemstone Buying Guide

How to evaluate, identify, select & care for colored gems

Second Edition

Renée Newman

International Jewelry Publications
Los Angeles _____

International Jewelry Publications
P.O. Box 13384
Los Angeles, CA 90013-0384 USA

(Inquiries should be accompanied by a self-addressed,
stamped envelope.)

Printed in Singapore

Library of Congress Cataloging-in-Publication Data

Newman, Renée.
   Gemstone buying guide: How to evaluate, identify,
select & care for colored gems / Renée Newman --
2nd ed
      p. cm.
Includes bibliographical references and index.
ISBN 0-929975-34-0
   1. Precious stones--purchasing. I. Title.

TS752.N49 2003
736'.2'0297--dc21

                                          2002035285

Cover photo: Colored gemstone suite from Cynthia Renée
Co.; photography by Robert Weldon.

Contents

Acknowledgments

I would like to express my appreciation to the following people for their contribution to the *Gemstone Buying Guide*:

Ernie and Regina Goldberger of the Josam Diamond Trading Corporation. This book could never have been written without the experience and knowledge I gained from working with them.

The American Gemological Laboratories and the Gemological Institute of America. They have contributed diagrams and information.

Eve Alfillé, Arthur Anderson, Kurt Baker, Charles Carmona, Paul Cory, Dr. Paul Downing, Pete Flusser, Andy Gero, Si and Ann Frazier, Mark Gronlund, Don Kay, Dr. Horst Krupp, Glenn Lehrer, Gail Levine, Peter Malnekoff, Cynthia Marcusson, Dr. Kurt Nassau, Pierre Paré, Howard Rubin, Sindi Schloss, Sherris Cottier Shank, Gerald Stockton and John S. White. They have made valuable suggestions, corrections and comments regarding the portions of the book they examined. They are not responsible for any possible errors, nor do they necessarily endorse the material contained in this book.

Gordon Aatlo, Eve J. Allfilé, Arthur Anderson, Asian Institute of Gemological Sciences, Peter Barr, Cap Beesley, David Clay Co., Color Masters Gem Corp, William Cox, Paula Crevoshay, Peggy Croft, Cynthia Renée Co., Tom DeGasperis, The Diamond Dove, Inc., Gary Dulac Goldsmith, Extrême Gioielli, Tom Harmon, Hubert Inc., Iteco, Inc., Richard Kimball, Korite International, Glenn Lehrer Designs, Majestic Opals, Mason-Kay, Inc., Michael Francis & Co., Burdett A. Milkens, Dan Miller, Fred Mouawad, Murphy Design, Pearce Design, Port Royal Antique Jewelry, Precious Gem Resources, Proprioro, Linda Quinn, Rox Designs, Mark Schneider, Sherris Cottier Shank, Libby Skamfer, Somos Creations, Wearable Sculpture by Trisko, Robert Weldon and Harry Winston Inc. Photos from them have been reproduced in this book.

Manoel Bernardes Ltd., Pete & Bobbi Flusser, Carrie Ginsburg Fine Gems, Mark Gronlund, Josam Diamond Trading Corporation, Danny & Ronny Levy Fine Gems, Overland Gems, Inc., Radiance International, Andrew Sarosi, Gerald Stockton, Timeless Gem Designs, Varna Platinum. Their stones or jewelry have been used for some of the photographs.

Ian & Amy Itescu, Josian Gattermeier and Donald Nelson. They have provided technical assistance.

Louise Harris Berlin. She has spent hours carefully editing the *Gemstone Buying Guide*. Thanks to her, this book is much easier for consumers to read and understand.

My sincere thanks to all of these contributors for their kindness and help.

7

Colored Gem Price Factors in a Nutshell

The following factors can affect the prices of colored gemstones:

♦ **Color**
♦ **Clarity** (degree to which a stone is free from flaws)
♦ **Transparency**
♦ **Shape**
♦ **Cutting style**
♦ **Cut quality** (proportions and finish)
♦ **Carat weight or stone size**
♦ **Treatment status** (untreated or treated? type and extent of the treatment)
♦ **Place of origin** (sometimes on certain high quality or rare stones with documentation)
♦ **Distinctness of phenomena** if present (e.g., stars, cat's-eyes, alexandrite's change of color)

Price Factors Explained

COLOR plays a major role in gem pricing, but its impact varies depending on the quality, size, variety and species of a gemstone. (A variety is a category within a gem species; e.g., amethyst and rock crystal are varieties of quartz, which is a species). Color has a greater effect on the price of blue sapphire, for example, than on blue topaz or yellow sapphire. Here are some guidelines:

In most cases, the stronger and more saturated the color, the more it is valued. For example, a strong green emerald can cost many times more than a lighter green emerald all other factors being equal.

In some cases, buyer/seller preferences impact prices more than the strength of the color. The Burma sapphire in figure 1.1 has a stronger blue color than the one from Sri Lanka in figure 1.2, yet some people in the trade would prefer the lighter blue color and consider it just as valuable. Both sapphires are beautiful and the fact that their color is natural and not the result of heat treatment makes them exceptional.

Fig. 1.1 Unheated Burma sapphire.
Photo & sapphire from Fred Mouawad.

Fig. 1.2 Unheated Sri Lankan sapphire.
Photo & sapphire from Fred Mouawad.

Fig. 1.3 Carved leopard skin jasper in a platinum and 18 karat gold butterfly brooch created by Eve J. Alfillé—an example of how an artist can transform an inexpensive brown, beige, and black stone into a museum-quality jewelry piece. *Design©by Eve J, Alfillé: photo by Matthew Arden*

In most cases, the more grayish, brownish or blackish a gemstone is, the lower its price. unless it's supposed to be black or brown. There's agreement in the trade that a blackish or grayish sapphire is far less valuable than a saturated blue one. Nevertheless, just because a stone is brownish or black, does not mean it's undesirable. Consider the jasper butterfly brooch in figure 1.3. Many people would reject a brown and black spotted stone like this one. Yet this is a stunning piece and the brown diamonds are the perfect accent for it.

The more rare a color is, the more it may be valued. In opal, red is the rarest color, so it's the most highly valued. In ammolite, blue is more rare so it's more prized. It's the rarity of the color, not just the color itself, that often determines prices.

Fig. 1.4 In opal, red is more rare than blue or green, so predominantly red opals like the one on the right are more highly prized. However, all three colors can be equally attractive as long as they are bright and intense. All of these black opals are of exceptionally fine quality. *Opals from Port Royal Antique Jewelry; photo by Harold and Erica Van Pelt.*

In most cases, the lower the quality of a stone, the less impact color has on price. Color has little influence on the price of low-grade translucent to opaque emeralds, but it has a significant effect on top-grade emeralds.

Low price does not necessarily mean low desirability. Light colored, low-priced gems can be quite attractive when well cut.

Chapter 4 has more guidelines on evaluating the color of gems and information about the effect of lighting on color. To learn more on how color affects the price of different gem varieties, see Chapters 11.

CLARITY is the degree to which a stone is free from flaws (inclusions and blemishes). Usually, the fewer, smaller and less noticeable the flaws, the higher the price, especially for higher priced gems such as rubies and emeralds. However there's a greater tolerance for flaws in colored gems than in diamonds, and prices are typically based on the visual appearance of colored stones rather than on clarity grades. There is no universally accepted grading system for colored gems. In some cases, flaws may be a welcome sign that a stone is natural and not treated nor lab-grown. For more information and photos on clarity, see Chapter 5.

Fig. 1.5 Inclusions in a sapphire (rutile needles). Their distinct, non-dissolved appearance indicates this stone has not been heat treated; its color is natural. *Photo by C. R. Beesley of AGL.*

TRANSPARENCY is the degree to which a gem is clear, hazy, translucent or opaque. (An opaque material does not allow light to pass through it; a translucent material resembles frosted glass.) Normally the higher the transparency the more valuable the stone. There are a few exceptions. Rubies and sapphires with microscopic particles which disperse the color, may be valued the same or sometimes a bit more than stones with a diamond-like transparency. For black opal, opaque stones tend to be more highly valued than those with a higher transparency.

Transparency can have a major impact on the value of a gemstone, especially for emerald, ruby, sapphire, opal, jade, star gems and cat's-eye gems. For example, a $20 Indian star ruby that's nearly opaque could possibly sell for as much as $400 if instead it were translucent or semi-transparent. A $10 sapphire that's nearly opaque could possibly sell for hundreds of dollars if it were transparent. See Chapter 5 for additional information.

Fig. 1.6 Emerald with a high transparency and noticeable inclusions.

Fig. 1.7 Less transparent emerald than the one in figure 1.6.

SHAPE is a gem's face-up outline (e.g., round or pear shaped). Color, clarity and transparency normally play a greater role in determining the price of colored gems than shape, cutting style and cut quality. Nevertheless, these latter three factors can affect the value of such stones.

The effect of shape on price varies depending on the seller, the gem variety, the stone weight, the stone quality and the demand for the shape. A *high-quality*, one-carat round ruby, for example, may cost 10% to 20% more than one with an oval shape because of greater demand and because there's more weight loss from the rough when cutting rounds. In small sizes and low qualities, the shape may have no effect on the price. The subject of shape pricing is complex. Simply remember to compare gemstones of the same shape and cutting style when evaluating gem prices.

The symmetry of the shape outline can also affect the per-carat price of large, high quality gems because symmetrical stones are desirable and may require more loss of weight from the rough.

CUTTING STYLE is the way in which a stone is cut or faceted. **Cabochon**s (unfaceted dome-shaped stones) and unfaceted beads are generally priced lower than faceted stones because they cost less to cut than faceted styles. Another reason cabochons are usually priced less is that they're often made from lower quality material that is unsuitable for faceting. Cabochon stones can also be of high quality, especially those found in antique jewelry.

Designer and trademarked cutting styles often sell for more than generic cuts of the same shape. The percentage impact tends to be the greatest for lower priced stones such as amethyst and blue topaz. A $20 well-cut standard oval blue topaz might sell for $100 if it had a unique faceting style or carved image created by a renowned cutter.

CUT QUALITY refers to the proportions and finish, also called **make**. This is a crucial factor because it affects the brilliance and color of gems, but its importance is not always reflected in the price of colored gems. Two of the main considerations of cut quality are:

1. **Do you see color all across the stone when you look at it face up?** Well-cut stones do not have large black areas nor do they have an obvious **window**—a pale, washed out area in the middle of stones that allows you to see right through them. In general, the larger the window, the poorer the cut. Even color throughout the stone indicates good cut quality.

Fig. 1.8 Print seen through a large window   **Fig. 1.9** Ruby with no window

2. **Are you paying for excess weight?** Suppose you have two stones with the same face-up size that are priced by carat weight. One is well cut and one has an overly deep and fat bottom and weighs twice as much. The overly deep stone would cost twice as much even though it has the same face-up size. In addition, it may be impractical for mounting and appear overly dark.

Keep in mind, however, that colored gems with good brilliance and color must often be cut deeper than diamonds. If colored stones are cut too shallow, they will have a window. See Chapter 6 for more information and photos on judging cut quality.

CARAT WEIGHT OR STONE SIZE is also an important value factor. In most cases, the higher the carat-weight category, the greater the per-carat price of a gem. A carat is a unit of weight equalling 1/5 of a gram.

Many translucent to opaque stones such as jade, malachite and chalcedony are sold by the piece or stone size, not by weight. Designer cuts may also be priced per piece, and colored stones under approximately half a carat are often priced according to millimeter size. Chapter 3 has additional information on carat weight.

TREATMENT STATUS includes three elements which can be important if you're spending a substantial amount of money on a gemstone:
1. **Is the stone treated or untreated?** Has the stone undergone a process other than cleaning, cutting or polishing to improve its natural appearance? Most colored stones are treated in some way by man. High quality untreated gems are usually the most highly valued because they're more rare and they're natural. However, an ugly untreated stone is typically worth less and harder to sell than one that's attractive and treated. That's why gems are treated.
2. **What treatment(s) did the stone undergo?** Not all treatments are equal. Some treatments, such as dyeing and cavity filling, have a more negative impact on value than others, like heat treatment, which is well accepted. Therefore it pays to find out what gem treatments were used on a gem before assessing its value. Chapter 8 discusses the various types of gem treatments.
3. **What is the extent of treatment?** This applies to clarity enhancements such as fracture filling. For example, practically all emeralds have tiny fractures. So it's customary to fill these fractures with an oil, wax or epoxy-type substance to mask them and sometimes increase durability. Assume that all emeralds you see for sale have been clarity enhanced, unless otherwise stated. Naturally a stone with a minor amount of filling is more valued than one with a substantial amount throughout the stone. Therefore gem labs now indicate on their documents the extent of the filling process, often by describing it as minor, moderate, significant, or none.

PLACE OF ORIGIN may refer to the country, area, or mine where a gem was mined. In most cases the source of colored gems does not matter—it's the quality that counts. However, for gems such as ruby, sapphire and emerald, origin can affect the price, provided the stone has a high quality and is accompanied by a lab report indicating a desired source. For example, good quality sapphires from Kashmir sell at a premium because of their rarity and exceptional color.

DISTINCTNESS OF PHENOMENA: Phenomena are unusual optical effects such as:
♦ **Chatoyancy** (cat's-eye): a band of reflected light in cabochons (gems with a domed, polished surface). It occurs when a strong light strikes needle-like inclusions or hollow tubes that are parallel within the stone. A cat's-eye effect may be seen on some chrysoberyl, emerald, aquamarine, apatite, quartz and tourmaline.
♦ **Asterism** (star): bands of reflected light crossing each other in the center to form a star with four, six or twelve rays. (See Chapter 7 for more information).
♦ **Adularescence**: a floating, shifting light effect caused by structural unevenness in moonstone, which scatters the light. On some high dome moonstones, it creates a cat's eye effect.

Gem Phenomena

Chatoyancy: Cat's-eye

Asterism: Indian star ruby

Adularescence: Moonstone

Iridescence: Ammolite.
Photo from Korite Intl.

Orient: Pearl

Change of Color: Alexandrite

Labradorescence: Labradorite

Aventurescence: sunstone

Play of Color: Opal

- ♦ **Aventurescence**: a glittery, sparkling effect caused by light reflecting off of minute platelike inclusions. In sunstone, the inclusions are usually platelets of copper or hematite, and in aventurine quartz they're a type of green mica.
- ♦ **Labradorescence**: a flash of color(s) in labradorite or spectrolite seen at certain viewing angles. It's caused by the interference of light through the layered structure of the labradorite.
- ♦ **Color change**: sometimes called the alexandrite effect. A change of color that occurs when the light source is changed. For example, an alexandrite, garnet or sapphire may appear purplish under incandescent light (e.g., light bulb), but green in daylight or fluorescent light.

Iridescent Gems

Fig. 1.19 Rainbow hematite. *Earrings by Eve Alfillé; photo by Matthew Arden.*

Fig. 1.20 Ammolite. *Pendant by Tom DeGasperis; photo by Shelly Smith.*

Fig. 1.21 Spectrolite. *Photo by Shelly Smith; pendant by Tom DeGasperis.*

Fig. 1.22 Fire agate. *Jewelry by Gary Dulac; photo by John Parrish.*

Fig. 1.23 Iris agate. *Photo by Tom Harmon.*

Fig 1.24 American freshwater cultured blister pearls and shell

♦ **Play of color**: a display of shifting colors in opal caused by clusters of microscopic silica spheres of uniform size, which break up the light into spectral colors.

♦ **Orient**: pearl iridescence. It results from the interference that occurs as light passes through layers of nacre. Orient may be a subtle combination of rainbow-like colors or of pink, blue, silver and sometimes green.

♦ **Iridescence**: a play of lustrous changing colors caused by the interference of light. The GIA (Gemological Institute of America) uses it to refer to the color phenomena of gems such as fire agate, rainbow agate and ammolite. Rainbow hematite also qualifies.

"Iridescence" has different meanings to different trade members. Some feel that a gem must show all colors of the rainbow to be classified iridescent; others require at last three colors, and still others would classify a solid red ammolite as iridescent as long as the quality of the color changes when the stone is moved. Many people extend the meaning of "iridescence" to describe the phenomena of gems such as opals and labradorite.

Trade members generally agree that the spectral (rainbow-like) effects seen in diamonds and demantoid garnet should be called "dispersion" or "fire" not iridescence. There seems to be agreement, too, that the colors must have a shifting quality rather than a static, fixed position like you'll see in banded agate or watermelon tourmaline (color zoning).

Fig. 1.25 Natural iridescence along the crack of an untreated diamond

Occasionally, the term "iridescent" is applied to gems with cracks displaying rainbow colors like those in the diamond of figure 1.25. However, stones like these are not considered to be "phenomenal gems" by appraisers, nor do gem texts list diamond as an iridescent gem species.

In general, the sharper and more obvious the phenomena, the more valuable the stone, all other factors being equal. However, don't expect the phenomena of natural stones to be as distinct as those on man-made stones. For example, the sharper and more noticeable a star, the more valuable the stone, unless it's a synthetic star. Natural stars are not as perfect as those on man-made stones.

Two Common Beliefs Which Warrant Review

1. **Color is just a matter of individual preference.** This is a common answer to the question, "What is the most valuable color?" The erroneous implication is that there are no trade standards for preferred colors. The pricing of colored gems is based on some universal principles regarding gem color—normally the less brown or gray present and the more saturated the color, the more valuable the stone. There are some exceptions. As already mentioned, the preferred strength of the blue in sapphires may vary depending on the nationality of the buyer.

For each gemstone, there is also a range of hues which command a higher price than others. Often, the closer gems are to a pure red, green or blue, the more valued their color is. Again there are exceptions, as is the case with greenish blue Paraiba tourmaline, which may sell for several thousand dollars per carat because of its rarity.

Even though your choice of color should be determined by what you like, you need to know how color is valued in order to accurately compare prices.

2. **Color is the most important factor for valuing colored stones**. Color is a major value factor, but it's not always the most important one. Suppose you have a fine $10,000-per-carat emerald. If it were translucent with the exact same color, it would be worth several times less, and transparency would be the main factor contributing to its lower value.

Fractures in tanzanite can have a significant effect both on its price and salability. On the other hand, light purple colors can be quite desirable even though they're priced lower than deep blues. If you examined the reject stones of colored-stone dealers, you'd find that most of the stones were rejected because of poor clarity and/or transparency. This doesn't mean clarity is more important than color; it just indicates that the importance of each grading factor varies from one stone to another. Consumers who focus on color and play down other value factors risk getting a poor buy. **When buying colored gems, remember—color is not everything,** even though it does play a substantial role. **Other factors can be equally important.**

Colored Gem Pricing

Some consumers think that dealers evaluate colored gems in a logical, analytical manner. Unlike diamond dealers, colored-gem dealers do not assign color and clarity grades according to a standardized grading system, nor do they list proportion measurements such as the angle of the top of the stone (crown angle).

Colored-gem dealers tend to evaluate gem quality as a whole rather than breaking it down to its constituent parts of color, clarity, transparency, proportions, etc. Their final judgments are usually more intuitive than logical. Non quality related factors also enter into their pricing strategies. Some of these price determinants are demand, form of payment, buyer's credit rating, amount purchased, competitors' prices. time of sale, the customer's eagerness to buy, the seller's need for money and his assessment of the buyer. Astute, knowledgeable buyers tend to be offered better prices.

Since you can't always count on prices to reflect the quality of gems, it's all the more important that you learn to make quality judgments yourself. The reason this book analyzes color and gem quality in terms of their component parts is to aid you in this process. Vague statements such as "look for color" are not helpful to consumers. However, when you learn how color elements and price factors affect the cost of a gem, it's easier for you to understand gem valuation. Your ultimate goal should be to reach the level where you can make quick comprehensive judgments about gem quality, as a dealer would. But like any other skill, this takes practice.

Independent gem lab documents and appraisals are recommended for verifying the identity, origin and treatment status of gemstones, especially for major purchases. Even experienced dealers realize the need for assistance from reputable gem labs when buying and selling gems. Consult the *Gem & Jewelry Pocket Guide* by Renée Newman for sample lab documents and information on choosing appraisers and gem labs,

Chapter 11 gives some broad price ranges for many of the gem varieties that are listed. Keep in mind that colored gem prices can change rapidly because of world events, new finds, or a depletion of sources. For example, the price of tanzanite almost doubled after the mines in Tanzania were flooded. Then they dropped significantly when there were reports of terrorist links to tanzanite. They rose again when the reports turned out to be unfounded.

For most gems, the price ranges are broad because of the variability in the quality. You can find very low-grade one-carat emeralds at public gem shows retailing for as low as $10. On the other hand, you can find top-grade one-carat emeralds retailing for as much as $10,000. Some extra fine emeralds weighing over eight carats have *wholesaled* for more than $15,000 per carat. In addition, within a given emerald quality type, there's a lot of price variation because of the numerous suppliers and geographic sources of emerald. Consequently it's impossible to indicate specific prices for emeralds. Keep in mind that a $1000 one-carat emerald, for example, may be a better buy than a $100 one-carat emerald. You must consider its quality and treatment status.

It's easier to be more specific about a gem such as benitoite, a transparent blue gemstone mined in California. There's only one distributer of faceted benitoite.

Use the price ranges in this book only as a general guideline of the relative values of gems. They may be obsolete when you read them, so do your own comparison shopping, and deal with knowledgeable sellers who will look after your interests. Don't become so focused on price that you overlook aesthetic features. Gems do not have to be of top quality to be acceptable, but they should meet *your* needs in terms of beauty and pizazz.

2

Shape & Cutting Style

When gemologists speak of a gem's **shape**, they usually mean its face-up outline. The most common gemstone shapes include the round, oval, square, triangle, pear, marquise, heart and **cushion**, a squarish or rectangular shape with curved sides and rounded corners. Gems can be any geometric shape or they may resemble things such as animals, bells, stars, the moon, etc. They can also be cut as abstract freeforms. Gem cutters try to select shapes and cutting styles which allow them to emphasize preferred colors and brilliance, minimize undesirable flaws, and/or get the maximum weight yield from the rough. In small calibrated sizes, there is a tendency to cut what jewelry manufacturers want, even when some shapes cause a greater weight loss. Standard sizes and shapes are required for mass-produced jewelry.

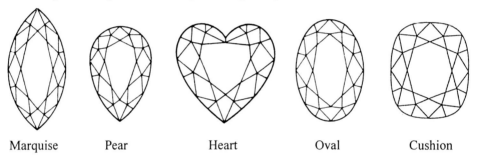

Marquise   Pear   Heart   Oval   Cushion

Cutting style refers to the way in which a stone is cut or faceted. An oval-shaped stone, for example, may just be rounded as a cabochon or it may have facets (polished surfaces with varying shapes) that are arranged in different styles. The term **emerald cut** has a double meaning. It indicates that the shape is square or rectangular with clipped-off corners and that the faceting style is a step cut, which has parallel rows of long, four-sided facets. A **radiant cut** has the same shape as an emerald cut but has facets similar to those of a round brilliant cut.

Fig. 2.1 Emerald cut

Fig. 2.2 Radiant cut

Sometimes rough gem material is not cut into any particular shape. Instead, it is just rounded and polished leaving the basic shape of the rough intact. This process is called **tumbling** and is generally used when the material doesn't warrant cutting. The rough pieces are tumbled in a rotating barrel with abrasives and water. As the stones slide against each other, they become smooth like pebbles in rivers that rub against sand and other pebbles. Tumbling is the simplest technique for fashioning gem rough. The resulting shape is described as **baroque**, which means "irregular in outline."

Fig. 2.3 Tumbled gemstones. *Ring & photo from Extrême Gioielli.*

Gemstone Terms Defined

To help you understand the sections on cutting styles, here are some basic terms:

Facets: The polished surfaces or planes on a stone. Normally they are flat, but some cutters are now creating stones with concave facets. Facets are intended to create brilliance in a gemstone.

Table: The large, flat top facet. It normally has an octagonal shape on a round stone.

Girdle: The narrow rim around the stone. The girdle plane is parallel to the table and is the largest diameter of any part of the stone.

Crown: The upper part of the stone above the girdle.

Pavilion: The lower part of the stone below the girdle.

Culet: The tiny facet on the pointed bottom of the pavilion, parallel to the table. Sometimes the point of a stone is called "the culet" even if no culet facet is present.

Fancy Shape: Any shape except round. This term is most frequently applied to diamonds.

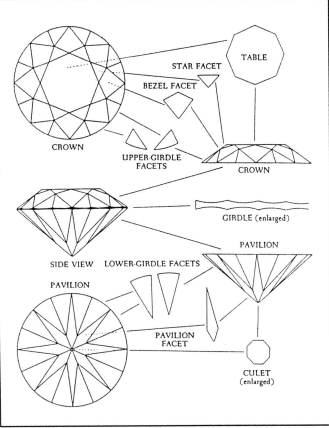

Fig 2.4 Facet arrangement of a standard round brilliant cut. *Diagram reprinted with permission from the Gemological Institute of America.*

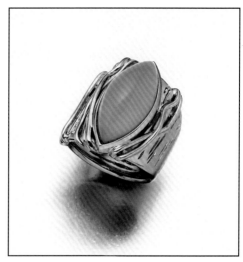

Fig. 2.5 Chrysocolla quartz cabochon cut by Noah Pearce of Pearce Design. *Photo by Ralph Gabriner.*

Fig. 2.6 Blue opal cabochon. *Ring designed by Tiziano Andorno; photo from Extrême Gioielli.*

Traditional Cutting Styles

Before the 1300's, gems were usually cut into unfaceted rounded beads or into cabochons (unfaceted dome-shaped stones). Colored gems looked attractive cut this way, but diamonds looked dull. Thanks to man's interest in bringing out the beauty of diamonds, the art of faceting gemstones was developed. At first, facets were added haphazardly, but by around 1450, diamonds began to be cut with a symmetrical arrangement of

Fig. 2.7 Table cut

facets. The first symmetrical style probably evolved out of the natural octahedral shape of some diamond crystals. Simply by flattening one point or cutting it off, a table facet was formed. This created a symmetrical style called the **table cut**, which had a crown, pavilion and nine facets (ten if there were a culet). More complex styles gradually emerged, and there were advances in cutting tools and technology. One of the most important developments was the introduction of the rotary diamond saw around 1900. By the 1920's, the modern round-brilliant cut had become popular.

As cutters discovered how faceting could bring out the brilliance and sparkle of diamonds, they started to apply the same techniques to colored stones. Today, gems are cut into the following basic styles:

Cabochon Cut Has a dome-shaped top and either a flat or rounded bottom. This is the simplest cut for a stone and is often seen in antique jewelry. Today this cutting style tends to be used for opaque, translucent, and star or cat's-eye stones, but transparent material is also used. Sometimes stones are cut as a cabochon on top and faceted on the bottom to add some brilliance.

Cabochon

Since the **cabochon** is the simplest style, it costs less to cut than faceted styles. Another reason cabochons are generally priced less is that they are often made from lower quality material that is unsuitable for faceting. Cabochon stones can also be of high quality, especially those found in antique jewelry.

Fig. 2.8 Square emerald-cut (step-cut) rubellite, which was cut to emphasize the color. *Ring and photo from Hubert Inc.*

Fig. 2.9 Emerald-cut aquamarines are often cut with more facets than emeralds, in order to bring out brilliance. *Ring and photo from Hubert Inc.*

Step Cut Has rows of facets that resemble the steps of a staircase. The facets are usually four-sided and elongated, and parallel to the girdle. One example is the **baguette**, a square-cornered, rectangular stone. If step-cuts have clipped-off corners, they're called **emerald cuts** because emeralds are often cut this way. This protects the corners and provides places where prongs can secure the stone. Emerald cuts are usually rectangular or square, but they can also be triangular. They tend to have more facets than baguettes. Light-colored emerald cuts often have more facets than shown in figure 2.11 below. The additional facets help maximize brilliance.

Fig. 2.10 Step-cut baguette

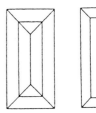

Fig. 2.11 Emerald cut

Brilliant Cut Has mostly 3-sided facets which radiate outward from the stone. Kite- or lozenge-shaped facets may also be present. The best-known example is the **full-cut round brilliant**, which has 58 facets. Ovals, pears, marquises, and heart-shapes can also be brilliant-cut. The **single cut**, which has 17 or 18 facets, is another type of brilliant cut. It may be found on small stones, often of low quality, or on imitations. Square stones cut in the brilliant style are called **princess cuts**. Triangular brilliant cuts are called **trilliants**. The princess and trilliant cuts were originally developed for diamonds because their brilliant-

Fig. 2.12 Single cut

21

Fig. 2.13 Princess-cut aquamarine. *Design by Emilio Minchiotti; photo and 18-karat white gold pendant from Extrême Gioielli.*

Fig. 2.14 Trilliant cut. *Pendant created by Mark Schneider; photo by Daniel Van Rossen.*

style facets create a greater amount of brilliance and sparkle than step facets do. Now the princess and trilliant cuts are becoming popular for colored stones.

Gemstone pendants or earrings are occasionally cut as **briolettes**. These have a tear-drop shape, a circular cross-section and brilliant-style facets (or occasionally rectangular, step-cut-style facets or else no facets).

Fig. 2.15 Ametrine briolette from Cynthia Renée Co. *Photo by Colladay.*

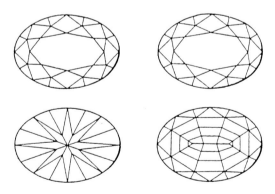

Fig. 2.16 Brilliant cut   **Fig. 2.17** Mixed cut

Mixed cut Has both step- and brilliant-cut facets. This is a popular faceting style for colored stones. The crown is brilliant-cut to maximize brilliance and hide flaws if present. The pavilion, on the other hand, is either entirely step cut or else has a

Fig 2.18 A spectral display of rounds in a variety of cutting styles all cut by Clay Zava of David Clay Co.
Top left: purple spinel and red spinel—Portuguese-cut pavilion with brilliant-cut crown
Third from top left: rhodolite—step-cut pavilion with a bufftop crown
Fourth from top left: rhodolite—Portuguese-cut pavilion with a bufftop crown
Left middle: pink spinel & left middle: orange spessartite garnet—checkerboard crown, step-cut pavilion
Right middle: pink-lavender spinel—Portuguese-cut pavilion with brilliant-cut crown
Right middle: orange spessartite garnet—"CD cone" (Clay Zava's name for the cut)
Lower far left: yellow chrysoberyl—Portuguese-cut pavilion with a bufftop crown
Middle: yellow chrysoberyl—Portuguese-cut pavilion with a brilliant-cut crown
Right: blue tourmaline—Portuguese-cut pavilion with a bufftop crown
Lower middle: blue tourmaline—Portuguese-cut pavilion with a brilliant-cut crown
Lower left: tsavorite—Checkerboard crown with a step-cut pavilion
Photo by Robert Weldon

Fig. 2.19 Faceted oval apatite beads (brilliant type facets) enhanced with Phoenician glass that is over 2000 years old. A removable blue-green boulder opal pendant is below the Phoenician glass. *Design copyright by Eve Alfillé; photo by Matthew Arden.*

combination of both step- and brilliant-type facets. The step facets allow cutters to save weight and bring out the color of the stone. Occasionally, the mixed cut is referred to as the **Ceylon cut.**

Bead (faceted & unfaceted)	Usually has a ball-shaped form with a hole through the the center. Most faceted beads have either brilliant- or step-type facets. Today, beads are generally made from lower-priced material. High-quality rubies and emeralds, for example, are usually faceted. It would be pointless to lower their weight and value by drilling holes through them.

Fig. 2.20 Step-cut bead

Fancy Cuts and Cutting Techniques

Many people use the term **fancy cut** to refer to almost any cut which is not a standard cabochon, brilliant-cut or step cut. One example is the **bufftop**, which is a gem that's faceted underneath with a cabochon top (see figure 2.18). Another example is the **Portuguese cut**, with brilliant style facets arranged differently than standard round brilliants.

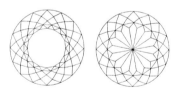

Fig. 2.21 Portuguese cut

Traditional step- and brilliant-cut stones have a large table facet on the crown. Contemporary cutters sometimes eliminate the table. They may facet squares or rectangles of similar size across the crown. This is called a **checkerboard cut** or **opposed-bar cut**, depending on the style. Another example of a faceting style without a table is the old-style **rose cut**, which has brilliant-style facets, a dome-shaped crown, a flat base and a round girdle outline. The **rose cut** may have originated in India and probably dates back to the fifteenth century. Rose cuts may also be cut with a pavilion.

Traditionally, the facets on gems have been flat. In recent years, some gem cutters have been experimenting with **concave facets.** By using concave shapes, faceters can create scalloped girdle outlines and increase brilliance. If light enters a gem and hits a flat facet, it is reflected in one

Some Fancy Cuts

Fig. 2.22 Portuguese-cut green tourmaline with a cushion shape

Fig. 2.23 Checkerboard-cut amethyst

Fig. 2.24 Step-cut half-barrel rhodolite. Also called an opposed-bar cut because the long pavilion facets go in opposite directions from those on the crown.

Fig. 2.25 Rectangular millennium-cut peridot. It has a step-cut crown and a pavilion with concave faceting.

Fig. 2.26 Rectangular opposed-bar cut tourmaline.

Fig. 2.27 Rose-cut *oro verde* ("green gold") quartz

All the rings, gemstones and photos on this page are from Hubert Inc.

Fig. 2.28 Citrine arrowhead concave faceted by Mark Gronlund

Fig. 2.29 Back view of the arrowhead in figure 2.28

Fig. 2.30 A golden beryl with an open table "halo cut" by Arthur Lee Anderson. *Photo by Robert Jaffe*

Fig. 2.31 Faceted blue topaz frames. *Jewelry by Burdett A. Milkens; photo by Sky Hall.*

direction. However, if it hits a curved surface, it is scattered in many directions, thereby magnifying the brilliance of the stone. Concave faceting normally takes about two to five times longer than conventional faceting. Consequently, stones with concave facets usually cost more than traditional cuts.

An **open table** is a concept that eliminates the crown and spreads the table so that the observer's eye is drawn into the interior of the stone. Both curved and flat facets may be used on

Fig. 2.32 Cameo. *Brooch & photo from Timeless Gem Designs.*

Fig. 2.33 Intaglio. *Photo & pendant from Timeless Gem Designs.*

the pavilion to create unusual patterns and optical effects when the stone is viewed face up. The "halo cut" in figure 2.30 is an example of this. Sometimes the entire center of the stone is cut out and there is neither a table nor a pavilion. See figure 2.31.

Sometimes gems are both faceted and carved. In such cases, they may be identified as either fancy cuts or carvings, which are discussed in the next section.

Carving

Carving is a specialized type of cutting which produces intricate designs and forms, not just flat facets or evenly curved surfaces. Any of the following art forms can be considered a carving:

Engraving: A shallow design cut into the surface of a stone. The overall shape and contour of the stone is changed very little.

Cameo: A stone, often banded chalcedony, with a design or picture cut in relief. The background is removed to expose the desired picture.

Intaglio: An engraved stone with a design cut shallow into its surface.

Sculpture: Stone cut as a three-dimensional object such as a figurine or bust.

Three-dimensional gemstone carving, also called loosely in the trade a **fantasy cut:** A stone with carved areas that may have some of the same characteristics as a traditional cut—it may be partially faceted or cabbed, and it may have a crown, girdle and pavilion. Gemstone carvers and faceters have similar goals—to bring out the brilliance and color of a gem. However, instead of just using small flat planes to accomplish this, gem carvers may also use grooves, curved planes, recessed areas and undercutting, which create a wide variety of effects.

In the past half century, many talented artists have become involved in gemstone carving because it offers the opportunity to work in a sculptural

Fig. 2.34 Fantasy-cut pink tourmaline by Bernd Munsteiner. *Ring designed, made and photographed by The Diamond Dove, Inc.*

27

Fig. 2.35 Carved gem flower brooch designed by Emilio Minchiotti. *Photo and brooch from Extrême Gioielli.*

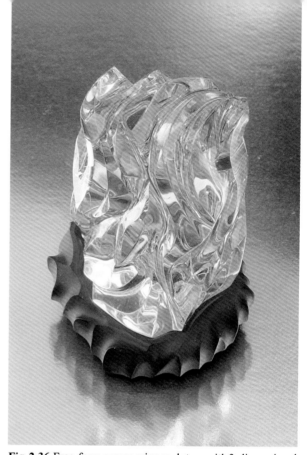

Fig. 2.36 Free-form aquamarine sculpture with 3-dimensional carving. *Designed and sculpted by Sherris Cottier Shank; photo by John McMartin.*

Fig. 2.37 Opal (54.07 ct) carved by Sherris Cottier Shank. *Pin/pendant by Paula Crevoshay ($13,200 retail); photo by Azad.*

Fig. 2.38 Carved Oregon sunstone. *Carving and photo by William Cox Gem Carvings.*

Fig. 2.39 Dendritic agate carved by Glenn Lehrer. *Photo by Azad.*

Fig. 2.40 Brazilian orange drusy agate with diamonds and a South Sea pearl. *Carved and photographed by Glenn Lehrer.*

Fig. 2.41 Imanja's bouquet carved by Lawrence Stoller—quartz, pearl, eight tourmalines, eight sapphires, bronze base (retail $21,000). *Piece by Paula Crevoshay; photo by Harold & Erica Van Pelt.*

Fig. 2.42 Smoky-quartz carving by Michael Dyber. *Pin and photo from Fred & Kate Pearce.*

Fig. 2.43 Chrysoprase carving (99.34 ct) by Glenn Lehrer. Paula Crevoshay created this piece, which is named "Butterfly Fairy Maiden" ($8,500). *Photo by Harold & Erica Van Pelt.*

Fig. 2.44 Natural crystal pendant designed by Tiziano Andorno. *Photo from Extrême Gioielli.*

Fig. 2.45 Drusy uvarovite. *Pendant with granulation hand-fabricated by Gary Dulac; photo by Azad.*

manner with beautiful color and fascinating optics. As a result, there are many new styles of cutting. Some modern carvers may cut a deep three-dimensional pattern into a stone with a crown, girdle and/or pavilion. The depth of cutting creates a play of light that is as important as the carving pattern itself. Some cutters may concentrate primarily on optical effects and others may depart entirely from recognized gemstone shapes, creating a gem that is entirely free-form.

Carvings are usually priced per piece instead of per carat. Their value depends on the skill and fame of the cutter, the type of material used, the time required to execute the design, the fame of the carving's owner(s), and their antique value if any. Custom-crafted, one-of-a-kind designs are naturally more expensive than those that are mass produced or machine-made.

Sometimes designers accept nature's handiwork and use natural crystals in their jewelry pieces (fig. 2.44). It's also becoming popular to use crystal accumulations called druse. See next section.

Drusy Gem Materials

Druse is a crust of tiny crystals on the surface of a rock or mineral. If the crust is garnet, for example, then it's called drusy (or druzy) garnet. Even though the base of the druse is normally not garnet, the combined base and crust are also called drusy garnet. The base is a natural part of the drusy material; it's *not* a backing that's glued to the crust. "Drusy" is also used as a noun, so "garnet drusy" equals "drusy garnet."

Before the 1990's, the only drusies jewelers used were quartz and agate (a member of the quartz group). But the burst of interest in drusy quartz in the late 1980's prompted discovery of drusy gem materials from other families such as uvarovite garnet, cobaltocalcite (see photo in the section on calcite) and psilomelane, a manganese ore which never before had been used in jewelry.

Most drusy material is untreated. Two exceptions are drusy black onyx, which is chalcedony that has been dyed black, and titanium drusy agate. It's coated with titanium in a vacuum chamber as a vapor deposition, producing sparkly shades of tanzanite blues.

Fig. 2.46 Drusy malachite. *Pendant by Tom De-Gasperis of Dancing Designs; photo, Shelly Smith.*

Fig. 2.47 Drusy dendritic agate. *Jewelry by Gary Dulac; photo by John Parrish.*

Fig. 2.48 Drusy chrysocolla quartz. *Pendant by Tom DeGasperis; photo by Shelly Smith.*

Fig. 2.49 Drusy psilomelane. *Pendant by Tom DeGasperis; photo by Shelly Smith.*

One important element in the evaluation of drusy is coverage. Crystal coverage relates to whether areas of the underlying host rock show. Top-grade drusy pieces have a sparkly, uninterrupted, thick pile of fine- to medium-grain bright crystals with highly saturated colors. Lower grades look dull and sometimes show areas of the base rock.

Clean drusy stones with water and a soft cloth and blot dry with a paper towel or cloth. It's best to avoid soaps and detergents because they can leave a film which may cling to the textured druse. In addition, avoid using brushes on coated drusies because they may damage the coating.

Today, designers and cutters are more creative than ever. They are transforming drusy stones and low priced gem materials such as quartz, chalcedony and blue topaz into distinctive jewelry pieces and spectacular works of art. Thanks to the greater emphasis on high-quality cutting, it's easier to find stones with pizazz than it was twenty years ago. For a better idea of what types of styles are now available, go to your local jeweler and ask to see some of the contemporary cuts and new gem materials. Don't forget your wallet. When you see how pretty these gems are, you'll want to own some.

3

Carat Weight

The term "carat" originated in ancient times when gemstones were weighed against the carob bean. Each bean weighed about one carat. Gem traders were aware, however, that the weights varied slightly. This made it advantageous for them to own both "buying" beans and "selling" beans.

In 1913, carat weight was standardized internationally and adapted to the metric system, with one carat equalling 1/5 of a gram. The term "carat" sounds more impressive and is easier to use than fractions of grams. Consequently, it is the preferred unit of weight for gemstones.

The weight of small stones is frequently expressed in **points**, with one point equaling 0.01 carats. For example, five points is the same as five one-hundredths of a carat. Contrary to popular belief, jewelers do not use "point" to refer to the number of facets on a stone. The following chart gives examples of written and spoken forms of carat weight:

Table 3.1

Written	Spoken
0.005 ct (0.5 pt)	half point
0.05 ct	five points
0.25 ct	twenty-five points or a quarter carat
0.50 ct	fifty points or a half carat
1.82 cts	one point eight two (carats) or one eighty-two

Note that "point" when used in expressing weights over one carat refers to the decimal point, not a unit of measure. Also note that "pt" can be used instead of "ct" to make people think for example, that a stone weighs 1/2 carat instead 1/2 of a point.

Size Versus Carat Weight

Sometimes in the jewelry trade, the term "size" is used as a synonym for "carat weight." This is because size and weight are directly related. However, as gems increase in weight, their size becomes less predictable. This means a 0.90-ct emerald, for example, may look bigger than a 1.05-ct emerald. Therefore, you need to consider stone measurements as well as carat weight when buying colored stones. You don't need to carry a millimeter gauge with you when you go shopping. Just start noting the different illusions of size that various stone shapes and measurements can create.

Fig. 3.1 The emerald (1.24 ct) looks almost twice the size of the ruby (1.11 ct), which has a similar weight and depth. The sapphire in the center weighs 2.73 cts, but it does not look double the size of the emerald. Since emeralds are not as dense as rubies and sapphires, emeralds appear larger.

You should also note that one gem species can have different measurements than another gem species of the same weight. For example, because of its higher density, a one-carat ruby is considerably smaller than a one-carat emerald. Rubies and sapphires are heavier (more dense) than diamonds and most colored stones. One major exception is garnet. Depending on the type, garnets may have a similar or greater density than corundum stones.

We can compare gem sizes by comparing their **specific gravity** (a ratio comparing the weight of a gem to an equal volume of water at 4°C). The specific gravity of emerald is about 2.72 whereas that of corundum (ruby and sapphire) is about 4.00. The specific gravity of diamond is about 3.52.

Effect of Carat Weight on Price

Most people are familiar with the principle, the higher the carat weight, the greater the value. However, they may not realize that a one-carat ruby, for example, is worth far more than several small rubies of similar quality with a total weight of one carat. This is because the supply of large rubies is more limited. So when you compare jewelry prices, besides noting the quality, you should pay attention to individual stone weights and **notice the difference between** the labels **1 ct TW** (one carat total weight) **and 1 ct** (the weight of one stone).

When comparing the cost of transparent gems, you should also start noting the **per-carat cost** instead of concentrating on the total cost of the stone. This makes it easier to compare prices more accurately, which is why dealers buy and sell most gems using per-carat prices. However, many opaque and translucent stones such as jade, malachite and chalcedony are sold by the stone or piece, not by weight. Designer cuts may also be priced per piece, and colored stones under about a half carat are often priced according to millimeter size. The following equations will help you calculate the per-carat cost and total cost of gemstones.

$$\text{Per-carat cost} = \frac{\text{stone cost}}{\text{carat weight}}$$

Total cost of a stone = carat weight x per-carat cost

The price/weight categories of colored gems vary from one dealer to another, so there's no point in listing any. Just be aware that carat weight can affect the per-carat value of gemstones and follow these two guidelines:

♦ Compare the per-carat prices of transparent gems instead of their total cost.

♦ When judging prices, compare stones of the same size, shape, quality and color.

Estimating Carat Weight

If you buy jewelry in a reputable jewelry store, you normally don't need to know how to estimate the carat weight of gems because the weight will be marked. However, if you buy jewelry at flea markets or garage sales, it is to your advantage to know how to estimate weight.

Appraisers estimate the weight of faceted gems by measuring their length, width and depth with a millimeter gauge (these are sold at jewelry supply stores). Then they calculate the weight with formulas such as the ones found in Table 3.2. The only accurate means of determining the weight of a stone is to take it out of its setting and weigh it. This, however, is not always possible or advisable.

Table 3.2 Weight Estimation Formulas for Faceted Gems	
Round	Diameter^2 x depth x S.G. x .0020
Oval	Diameter^2 x depth x S.G. x .0021 (Average out length and width to get diameter)
Rectangular Cushion	Diameter^2 x depth x S.G. x .00235 (Average length and width to get diameter)
Square Emerald Cut	Length x width x depth x S.G. x .0023
Rectangular Emerald Cut	Length x width x depth x S.G. x .0027
Square (with corners)	Length x width x depth x S.G. x .0025
Rectangular Baguette	Rectangular Baguette
Pear	Length x width x depth x S.G. x .0020
Marquise	Length x width x depth x S. G. x .0021
Heart	Length x width x depth x S.G. x .00195

Note: S.G. = Specific Gravity. The specific gravity of the major gems is given in Chapter 11, "Gemstone Descriptions." The above formulas are based on stones with medium girdles, no pavilion bulge, and well-proportioned shapes. Thick girdles may require a correction of up to 10%. Bulging pavilions may require a correction as high as 18%. The correction for a poor shape outline can be up to 10%. For further information on weight estimation, consult the *Complete Handbook of Weight Estimation* by Charles Carmona.

4

Judging Color

Depending on whom you talk to, sherry-colored topaz is either yellow, orange, yellowish brown or reddish. That's because people have different opinions as to what is the color of sherry. Color terms like "sherry" "champagne" and "cognac" are great for displays and advertisements, but they're not appropriate for lab reports, appraisals and serious gemological texts because they don't give you a good visual idea of gem color.

Expressions like "grass green" are not much better. This term has been used in gemological literature to describe the color of peridot, alexandrite viewed outdoors, and fine emerald. That's understandable because grass comes in a wide range of greens. Most grasses, however, tend to be grayish or brownish, so it would be difficult to find grass with a top-grade emerald color.

For a more precise and accurate description of gems, it's helpful to divide color into the three components below. There are other ways to break down color; but this book uses the system employed by the Gemological Institute of America (GIA) and the American Gemological Laboratories (AGL).

Hue   Refers to the basic colors of blue, green, yellow, orange, red, purple and violet as well as transition colors like bluish green and yellowish green. (Sometimes people are not sure of the difference between purple and violet. Violet falls between blue and purple. Purple is between red and violet so it is redder than violet.) Brown, black, gray and white are not considered to be hues.

Lightness/darkness (Tone)   Refers to the amount of color. The lightest possible tone is colorless. The darkest is black. **Tone** is another word for the degree of lightness or darkness. We'll describe tone in this book by the following terms:

very light	medium dark
light	dark
medium light	very dark
medium	

Amount of gray or brown present   Refers to the color purity. The GIA calls this component **saturation**. The American Gemological Laboratories calls it **intensity**. "Intense," "strong," and "saturated" are terms used to describe colors with a minimal amount of gray or brown masking the hue. Otherwise they may be identified as grayish, slightly grayish, very slightly brownish, etc.

The terms **saturation** and **intensity** have other meanings as well. When some dealers describe the color of a stone as saturated, they mean it has both a high purity and good depth of color (tone). To them, a light pure color is neither saturated, nor intense. "Saturation" sometimes only refers to the tone of pure colors. This is how it is used in GemDialogue, a color reference system used by many appraisers.

A term such as "intense medium green" is less ambiguous than expressions like "grass green" and "sherry-colored." However, it's not as precise as using a color master stone or color sample as a reference point for describing gem color. Not everyone has the same visual image of intense medium green. So keep in mind that the color descriptions in this book are general, not precise. Nevertheless, they're better than "grass green," "cornflower blue" and "pigeon-blood red," terms which have often been used to describe the top color of emerald, sapphire and ruby.

Evaluating Gemstone Color

Even though it's debatable as to which are the most valuable hues and tones, gem dealers agree that pure, vivid colors are far more desirable than dull, muddy ones. In most high-quality stones, the bright areas of color should not look grayish or brownish.

Judging the **lightness or darkness** of a faceted gemstone is difficult because it doesn't display a single, uniform tone. It can have light and dark areas which become more apparent as you rock the stone in your hand. To judge the tone of a faceted gem, examine it face-up and answer the following questions:

♦ What is your first overall impression of the tone? How does it compare to that of other stones of the same variety? Use words such as "light" and "medium light" to describe tone, but keep in mind that the tonal boundaries of these terms can vary from one person and grading system to another. In most cases, medium to medium-dark tones are more valued than light and very dark tones.

The depth of color can play a major role in the price of gems. For example, a pure deep-green emerald selling for $5000 might be worth less than $100 if it were very light green. There's nothing inherently wrong, however, with light-green emeralds. In fact, they can be quite flattering to people who look good in pastel colors. It's just that there is a much greater demand for deep-green emeralds and their supply is more limited.

♦ Do you see near colorless, washed-out areas in the stone? This is a symbol of insufficient color, poor cutting or both.

♦ What percentage of the stone looks black? If more than 90% of a stone is blackish, gem dealers would classify it as undesirable, assuming that the stone is not black onyx or some other normally black stone. Many low-priced sapphires look black. Good sapphires are blue.

The GIA refers to the dark black or gray areas seen through the crown of faceted gems as **extinction**. The amount of extinction you see depends on the tone, the cut, the type of lighting and the distance of the light from the stone. Light-colored, shallow-cut stones normally show less extinction than those which are dark-toned or deep-cut. As the light source gets broader, more diffused, and/or closer to stones, they display less extinction and more color.

Fig 4.1 Sapphires with colors ranging from good (left) to low grade (right) viewed on a white paper with a desk lamp. The sapphire on the right is too black, and the sapphire next to it looks washed out because of an undesirable "window" (a see-through effect caused by poor cutting).

Fig. 4.2 Burmese ruby with excellent color. *Ring and photo from Color Masters Gem Corp.*

Fig. 4.3 Sapphire with excellent color. *Jewelry and photo from Harry Winston, Inc.*

Fig. 4.4 Tanzanite with excellent color from Carrie G. Fine Gemstones

Fig. 4.5 Emerald with excellent color. *Jewelry and photo from Harry Winston, Inc.*

Judging the **hue** of a stone is just as hard as judging the tone. The different tones within it are distracting. Moreover, it may be a blend of two or three colors. When you look at the stone from different directions while moving it, you can see the different colors. This is due to certain optical properties of the stone, which are discussed in Chapter 11, Gemstone Descriptions. This chapter also indicates the most valued hues for many of the important gem varieties. To determine the hue, look for the dominant color in the face-up view. Go with your first overall impression. Keep in mind that the most expensive hues are not necessarily the ones which will look best on you. If you don't plan to resell your stone, there's no need to base your choice of hue on trade preferences. Just choose the color you like best and that fits your budget.

Fig. 4.6 Top grade ammolite. *Pendant designed by Oriana Ngan; photo from Korite International.*

Fig. 4.7 Intermediate grade ammolite. *Pin by Fred and Kate Pearce; photo by Ralph Gabriner.*

Fig. 4.8 Low grade ammolite. *Pin by Fred and Kate Pearce; photo by Kate Pearce.*

Evaluating the color of gems with color phenomena is more complex than for other gems. The ammolite stone on the left is of exceptional quality because it has a brilliant and diverse color display (including the rare blue). Also, unlike most ammolite stones, there are hardly any dark areas or lines interrupting its color.

How to Examine Color

When selecting a gemstone, follow these steps:

♦ Clean the stone with a soft cloth if it's dirty. Dirt and fingerprints hide color and brilliance.

♦ Examine the stone face up against a variety of backgrounds. Look straight down at it over a non-reflective, white background and check if the center of the stone is pale and washed out. (This is undesirable). Then look at it against a dark background. Do you still see glints of color or does most of the color disappear? Also, check how good the stone looks next to your skin.

♦ Examine the stone under direct light and away from it. Your stone won't always be spotlighted as you wear it. Does it still look colorful out of direct light? It should if it's of good quality.

♦ Look at the stone under various types of light available in the store. For example, check the color under an incandescent light-bulb, fluorescent light, and next to a window. If you're trying to match stones, it's particularly important to view them together under different lights. Stones that match under one light source may be mismatched under another.

♦ Every now and then, look away from the stone(s) and glance at other colors and objects to give your eyes a rest. When you focus too long on one color, your perception of it is distorted.

♦ Rotate the stone and examine it for **color zoning**—the uneven distribution of color. When the color is uneven or concentrated in one spot, this can sometimes decrease the stone's value. It can also present a problem if the stone is recut. The color may become lighter. Obvious color zoning is most serious when visible in the face-up view of a stone.

♦ Compare the stone side by side with other stones of the same variety. Color nuances will be more apparent.

♦ Make sure you're alert and feel good when you examine stones. If you're tired, sick, or under the influence of alcohol or drugs, your perception of color will be impaired.

How Lighting Affects Gemstone Color

Visualize how different the colors of a snow-capped mountain are at sunrise and midday. This difference is due to the lighting, not to a change in the mountain itself. Likewise, the color of a gemstone will change depending on the lighting.

The whitest, most neutral light is at mid morning and mid afternoon. Besides adding the least amount of color, this light makes it easier to see the various nuances of color. Consequently, you should judge gemstone color under a daylight-equivalent light. Neutral fluorescent bulbs approximate this ideal, but some of these lights are better than others. Three that are recommended are the Duro-Test Vita light, GE Chroma 50 or Sylvania Design 50. Even though gemstones are graded under daylight-equivalent light, many stones such as rubies and emeralds are often displayed and look their best under incandescent light (light bulbs).

When you shop for gems, your choice of lighting will probably be limited. Use the information below to help you compensate for improper lighting when you judge color. Some of the data is from "The Effects of Lighting on Gemstone Colors" by Howard Rubin.

Type of Lighting	Effect of Lighting on Gem Color
Sunlight	At mid-morning and mid-afternoon, it normally has a neutral effect on the hue. At midday, it adds blue, making stones appear more bluish or violetish. Late in the day, it adds red, making gems look more red, orange or yellow.
Incandescent light bulbs, penlights and candlelight	Add red. Red colors are intensified, warm colors appear more alike, grayish colors may look brownish, and green may look darker and a bit more yellowish or less bluish.
Fluorescent lights	Depends on what type they are. Most intensify blue colors. Warm white tubes add yellow.
Halogen spotlights	Add sparkle and usually add yellow.
Light under an overcast sky or in the shade	Adds blue. Reds appear more purplish, greens and purples look more bluish, yellows look greener, blues appear stronger.

Some stones such as alexandrite, tanzanite and color-change garnet and sapphire can change color under different lights. These stones should also be evaluated under an incandescent lamp (a pen-light is not a large enough light source). If a written appraisal is being done on the stone, the color under both fluorescent and incandescent light should be noted. Your final judgment of a gemstone, however, should be based on its appearance in daylight equivalent light.

When buying gems remember to consider the lighting. It has a major impact on gem color.

5

Judging Clarity & Transparency

Clarity and transparency are important value factors for gems, sometimes even more important than color. Consider, for example, emeralds or sapphires. No matter how grayish, brownish, and/or light-colored they are, they're still gems if they are transparent and **eye-clean** (free of flaws visible to the unaided eye). The term **clean** by itself can mean that a stone is of high clarity. However, if they are opaque and filled with deep cracks and eye-visible flaws, they're industrial grade stones, even if they have a desirable color.

Some gems are more likely to have flaws than others. Emeralds, for example, typically have some eye-visible flaws. Aquamarine, on the other hand, is normally eye clean. As a result, there is a greater tolerance for noticeable flaws in emerald than in aquamarine. Two other gems that usually have eye-visible flaws are ruby and alexandrite. Some of the stones that typically have a high clarity like aquamarine are blue zircon, citrine, green tourmaline, green and yellow chrysoberyl, yellow sapphire, kunzite, topaz and tanzanite. Some colored gems that fall between these high- and low-clarity groups include amethyst, blue tourmaline, blue sapphire, garnet, iolite, peridot, spinel and zircon that is green, orange or red.

Before continuing this chapter, let's explain some basic terminology. **Clarity** is the degree to which a stone is free from flaws. Gemologists call flaws within a stone **inclusions**. Flaws on a stone's surface are **blemishes**. A general term for inclusions and blemishes is **clarity characteristics**. In this book, "flaw" is often used because it is shorter and clearer. Some trade members believe the use of the word "flaw" creates customer resistance to gems. When inclusions and blemishes are properly explained, it doesn't matter what they are called. Customers will learn to accept them as a normal characteristic of natural gemstones.

Even though flaws often have a negative impact on value, their presence can be positive. Flaws are identifying

Fig. 5.1 The inclusions in this Montana moss agate increase its value. It's on display at the Montana Agate Museum in Savage, Montana. *Photo and bola tie by Tom Harmon.*

Figs 5.2 & 5.3 Two views of a ruby with undesirable inclusions, including a long crack & concentrations of red dye

Fig. 5.4 The barely visible, "silk" inclusions in this ruby are a welcome sign that its rare color is natural, and not the result of heat treatment. *Photo and ruby from Precious Gem Resources.*

marks that can help you identify your stone at any time. They are especially important as evidence that your stone is natural. Jewelers and dealers are suspicious of flawless rubies, emeralds and alexandrites because that's usually a sign the stone is synthetic (man-made). Certain inclusions, such as silk, help prove that a gem is untreated. Inclusions can also increase the value of a stone by helping prove that it's from a location such as Kashmir. (Certain places have a reputation for producing top-quality gemstones). Sometimes inclusions add value to a gem simply because of their beauty as in figure 5.1. With colored gems, it doesn't matter whether a stone is flawless or not; what matters is the types of flaws that are present and whether they have a negative impact on appearance and/or durability.

Transparency

Transparency is the degree to which light passes through a material so that objects are visible through it. Transparency and clarity are interlinked because flaws can block the passage of light. Gemologists use the following terms to describe gem transparency.

♦ **Transparent**—objects seen through the stone look clear and distinct.

♦ **Semitransparent**—objects look slightly hazy or blurry through the stone.

♦ **Translucent**—objects are vague and hard to see. Imagining what it is like to read print through frosted glass will help you understand the concept of translucency.

♦ **Semitranslucent** or **semi-opaque**—a small fraction of light passes through the stone, mainly around the edges.

♦ **Opaque**—virtually no light passes through the stone. When classifying the transparency of a gem variety, "opaque" is considered to refer to specimens of ordinary thickness, because in thin slices most "opaque" substances transmit some light.

Occasionally, **near transparent** is used as a category between transparent and semitransparent. The most transparent specimens of jade and opal can fit in this category as well as many high-quality emeralds and rubies.

Another word that refers to transparency is **texture**. AGL (American Gemological Laboratories) in New York applies this term to fine particles which interrupt the passage of light in a material. The finely divided particles are not detrimental to the durability of a stone, but they can have an adverse effect on its appearance. Yet texture is not always a negative factor. The texture within Kashmir sapphire, for example, gives it a prized velvety appearance. AGL, on its lab documents, describes the texture (transparency) of colored stones as follows:

♦ Faint texture: very slightly hazy
♦ Moderate texture: cloudy
♦ Strong texture: translucent
♦ Prominent texture: semitranslucent or opaque

Texture can also refer to the fineness of the tiny crystal components of rock-like gem materials. For example, jade can have a fine to coarse texture depending on the size of its interlocking crystal constituents, which are ideally microscopic.

Dealers often use other terms to designate gem transparency, some of which are:

♦ crystal (highly transparent)   ♦ cloudy
♦ highly transparent   ♦ looks like soap
♦ milky   ♦ sleepy (has low transparency)

Jade dealers often use **translucency** instead of the term "transparency." Dealers of opal, another opaque to near transparent gem, generally prefer to use "transparency." For the sake of consistency, this book uses "transparency" for all gems when referring to how easily light can pass through them. It's easier to understand gemstone evaluation when the same terminology is used for every gemstone. Whether a gem is traditionally considered as transparent or translucent, transparency can play a major role in its value. Don't overlook this when comparing the prices of gemstones.

Gemstone Inclusions

Opinions differ as to how various clarity features should be classified. Some feel the term "inclusion" should be reserved for foreign matter within a stone. This book uses a broader definition, which is found in the GIA gemstone courses: "**Inclusions** are characteristics which are entirely inside a stone or that extend into it from the surface." The GIA defines **blemishes** as "characteristics confined to or primarily affecting the surface."

As you examine stones under magnification, you'll probably wonder what inclusions you are looking at. Listed below are gemstone inclusions found in colored stones:

♦ **Crystals** are solid mineral inclusions of various shapes and sizes. Minute crystals that look like small specks under 10X magnification are sometimes called **pinpoints** or **grains**. Crystals lower the clarity, but they can also turn a stone into a collector's item if they are unusual and attractive. The larger and more visible the crystals are, the more they impact the clarity.

Fig. 5.5 Crystal inclusions in a light blue sapphire cabochon

Fig. 5.6 A crystal and fingerprint inclusion in tanzanite

- **Negative crystals or voids** are hollow spaces inside a stone that have the shape of a crystal. They often resemble solid crystals, so for purposes of clarity grading, they're just called "included crystals."

- **Needles** are long, thin inclusions that are either solid crystals or tubes filled with gas or liquid, which are called **growth tubes**.

- **Clouds** are hazy or milky areas in a stone. Most clouds are made up of crystals too tiny to see individually under ten-power magnification. When clouds are large and dense, they diminish transparency.

- **Silk** in gemstones consists of very fine fibers of minerals such as rutile (titanium dioxide). It can also be made of mineral grains arranged in straight rows. These fibers or rows intersect and resemble silk, hence the name. Well-formed silk can be proof that a stone was not heat-treated to improve its color. Very high temperatures tend to dissolve it and make it look fuzzy or dot-like. Since untreated stones tend to be more valued than treated ones, the presence of clear, well-formed silk can be a welcome sign.

- **Cracks** of various sizes are not uncommon. They may also be called **fractures, fissures** or **breaks**. When they're straight and flat, they're called **cleavages**. Because of their appearance, cracks are sometimes called **feathers**. Normally, you need not worry about cracks if they are small. However, if they are deep or long, they can threaten the durability of the stone. The location of the cracks is also important. Surface cracks on the table of a stone have a negative impact on value. A crack in the center of the stone is much easier to see with the naked eye than one close to the edge.

- **Halos** are circular fractures surrounding a crystal. These structures generally result from tension created by the growth of the crystal inside the halo or by heat treatment.

- **Fingerprints** are partially healed cracks. Many colored gems grow from a mineral solution, and if they split during formation, the solution can fill the cracks and let them grow back together. During this healing process, stray drops of liquid are sealed in and form patterns that look like human fingerprints.

♦ **Fluid inclusions** are hollow spaces filled with fluid. They occur in random shapes and sometimes are so dense that the stone may look milky.

Fluid inclusions are classified into three types: **single-phase**, a void containing only fluid; **two-phase**, a liquid and a gas or two nonmixable liquids; and **three-phase**, a liquid, a gas and a solid. These inclusions can provide clues about the origin of a stone. Colombian emeralds, for example, are noted for their jagged-edged, three-phase inclusions which contain a salty liquid, gas bubble(s) and salt (halite) crystal(s). Indian emeralds often have parallel two-phase inclusions.

Fig. 5.7 A three-phase inclusion in a Colombian emerald

♦ **Growth or color zoning** refers to an uneven distribution of color in a stone. If the different color zones look like bands, they are called **growth or color bands**. This is usually visible under 10X magnification. If visible to the unaided eye, color zoning may be undesirable

♦ **Cavities** are holes or indentations extending into a stone from the surface. Cavities can result when solid crystals are pulled out of a stone or when negative crystals are exposed during the cutting process.

♦ **Chips** are notches or broken off pieces of stone often along the girdle edge or at the culet.

Gemstone Blemishes

♦ **Scratches** are straight or crooked lines scraped on a stone. Since they can be polished away, they don't have much of an effect on the clarity.

♦ **Pits** are tiny holes on the surface of a stone that often look like white dots.

♦ **Abrasions** are rough, scraped areas usually along the facet edges of a stone. They are seen more often on colored stones than on a diamond, due to the diamond's exceptional hardness.

Examining Gemstones for Clarity

To examine a stone for clarity you need a ten-power magnifier, a lint free cloth and a light source with a translucent shade or with a bulb that's frosted—not bare. An ordinary fluorescent desk lamp will do. Tweezers or a stoneholder is also helpful. Jewelers often use a hand magnifier called a loupe. For those interested in owning a loupe, the business section of the phone book has stores listed under *Jewelers' Supplies & Findings.* First verify that they have a fully corrected, ten-power, triplet loupe. The loupe salesman or a jeweler can show you some ways of holding

Fig. 5.8 A 10-power triplet loupe

45

and using it and help you select the model that is the most comfortable and clear. Plan on paying at least $25 for a good loupe. Cheaper types, which are not fully corrected, tend to distort objects.

When using a ten-power loupe, hold it about 1/2 to 1 inch (13-25 mm.) away from the stone to bring it into focus. If you're examining a large stone, hold the loupe close to one eye (about 1 or 2 inches or 25-50 mm. from the eye) keeping both eyes open. The closer the loupe is to your eye, the greater your field of vision will be.

Often it's easier for lay people to examine stones through a microscope. Many jewelers own microscopes and encourage their customers to use it when purchasing gemstones.

When you have the necessary equipment, you can proceed as follows:

♦ **Clean the stone**. Otherwise, you may think dirt and spots are inclusions. Usually rubbing it with a lint-free cloth is sufficient. If you're examining jewelry at home, it may have to be cleaned with water. (See Chapter 11 for cleaning instructions.) Professional cleaning might also be necessary. Avoid touching the stone with your fingers as fingers can leave smudges.

♦ **Examine the entire stone without magnification**. (However, if you require eyeglasses for reading, you'll need to wear them when examining gems.) One of the main criteria for assessing the clarity of colored gems is the visibility of the inclusions with the naked eye. Looking at the stone first with a loupe or microscope can mislead you into believing inclusions are eye visible when they aren't, because your mind has a tendency to see what it expects to see. So check to see if there are any noticeable flaws before using magnification. If you are looking at a good topaz, aquamarine or tanzanite, you shouldn't see any. A good ruby or emerald, on the other hand, is likely to have eye-visible inclusions. However, the fewer flaws it has, the higher its value.

♦ **Check the overall transparency of the stone**. If your goal is to buy a high-quality transparent gemstone, avoid cloudy or opaque stones.

♦ **Look at the stone from several angles**—top, bottom, sides. Even though top and centrally-located inclusions are the most undesirable in terms of beauty, those seen from the sides or bottom of a stone can affect its price or durability.

♦ **Look at the stone also with light shining through it from the side** (transmitted light). This will help you see flaws inside the stone. It will also help you judge transparency.

♦ **Look at the stone with light shining on it from various angles**—above it, through the sides, and reflected off the surfaces. Overhead illumination will help you determine what the blemishes and inclusions look like under normal lighting conditions. Light transmitted through the sides will highlight inclusions and will usually make them more visible. Light reflected off the surface will help you identify surface cracks and blemishes.

♦ **When you judge clarity, compare stones of the same type**. Emeralds, for example, should be compared to emeralds, not to other gems, which typically have a higher clarity. Tanzanite, a transparent, clean stone, should be compared to other tanzanites, not to sapphire, which tends to be more included.

♦ **Keep in mind that light-colored stones should have a better clarity than darker ones.** In lighter stones, inclusions are easier to see. Dark colors often mask flaws.

Figs. 5.9 & 5.10 Two views of an emerald with liquid inclusions and fractures—one in darkfield illumination under 10-power magnification and another in overhead lighting with less magnification.

♦ **Remember that prongs and settings can hide flaws.** If you're interested in a stone with a high clarity, it may be best for you to buy a loose stone and have it set.

♦ **Keep in mind that your overall impression of a stone's clarity can be affected by the stones it is compared to.** A stone will look better when viewed next to one of low clarity than next to one of high clarity. To have a more balanced outlook, try to look at a variety of qualities.

How Lighting Can Affect Your Perception of Clarity

You should judge the clarity of colored stones using overhead lighting both with and without magnification. A loupe (hand magnifier) or a microscope can help you see potentially damaging flaws that might escape the unaided eye.

When people use microscopes to judge clarity, they usually examine the stones with a type of lighting called **darkfield illumination**. This is a diffused lighting that comes up diagonally through the bottom of the stone. (A frosted or shaded bulb provides **diffused** light, a clear bulb does not.) In this lighting, tiny inclusions and even dust particles will stand out in high relief. As a result, the clarity of the stone appears worse than it would under normal conditions (figures 5.9 to 5.12 provide examples of this).

Overhead lighting is above the stone (not literally over a person's head). It is reflected off the facets whereas darkfield lighting is transmitted through the stone. When looking at jewelry with the unaided eye, you normally view it in overhead lighting. However, if you ask salespeople to show you a stone under a microscope, it is unlikely that they will use its overhead lamp. Instead they may only have you view the stone under darkfield illumination.

When judging colored-stone clarity under magnification, you should use overhead lighting for the following reasons:

♦ **Dealers use overhead lighting when pricing gems**. They typically examine stones under a fluorescent lamp with and without a loupe (usually 10-power).

Fig. 5.11 An iolite in overhead light. From the standpoint of appearance, the clarity is not bad. However, large cracks in the stone threaten its durability.

Fig. 5.12 Darkfield illumination turns the hardly noticeable cracks into distracting inclusions. Ten-power magnification through a microscope was used for this stone in both photos.

♦ **Overhead illumination is a natural way of lighting which does not exaggerate flaws.** It therefore helps you make a fair assessment of a stone's appearance.

♦ **Overhead lighting does not hide brilliance.** The prime reason for looking at gems through loupes and microscopes is to see their beauty and brilliance magnified. Darkfield illumination masks brilliance. Consequently, it prevents you from making an accurate global assessment of a gem under magnification.

After using overhead lighting, you should also view stones under darkfield illumination. It highlights inclusion details which are useful for detecting synthetics, treatments, and place of origin. With emeralds, for example, darkfield illumination can help you determine the depth of cracks, the type of filling present in fractures, and the extent to which an emerald may have been treated to hide cracks. In summary, darkfield lighting is a useful diagnostic aid, but it can be misleading when used for judging the clarity of colored stones.

Do We Need Grades to Evaluate Clarity and Transparency?

The diamond industry has a standardized system for grading clarity based on a system developed by the GIA. Ten-power magnification is used. The advantage of having this system is that buyers can communicate what they want anywhere in the world. In addition, written appraisals and quality reports are more meaningful.

One of the drawbacks of the diamond grading system is that it has sometimes caused buyers to become so focused on color and clarity that they overlook brilliance and cut. Another drawback is that it has led people to judge stones by grades rather than with their eyes. No grade or lab report can give a full picture of what a stone looks like. In addition, grades are often misrepresented. Without examining a stone under magnification, one cannot tell if a grade has been inflated.

Even though clarity grading systems have been developed for colored stones, there is no one standardized system. Even when a single system is used, there can be a wide variation in how grades are assigned by appraisers, mainly because the way in which transparency is incorporated into the system may differ. Therefore, it's best for you to ask appraisers what their grades mean. Grades are helpful for documentation purposes, but you don't need them to judge clarity and transparency.

6

Judging Cut Quality

C ut plays a major role in determining the value of colored gems because it affects their color and clarity as well as their brilliance. For example, a stone that is cut too shallow can look pale and lifeless, and it can display flaws that would normally not be visible to the naked eye.

The term **cut** is sometimes confusing because it has a variety of meanings. Jewelers use it to refer to:

♦ The **shape** of a gemstone (e.g. round or oval)

♦ The **cutting style** (e.g. cabochon or faceted, brilliant or step cut, single or full cut)

♦ The **proportions** of a stone (e.g. pavilion depth, girdle thickness)

♦ The **finish** of a stone (e.g. polishing marks or smooth flawless surface, misshapen or symmetrical facets)

The proportions and finish are also called the **make** of the stone. Proportions and how they affect the appearance of emeralds and tanzanites will be the focus of this chapter. Shape and cutting style were discussed in Chapter 2. Finish won't be discussed because it normally does not have much of an effect on the price of colored stones. If there is a problem with the finish, it can usually be corrected by repolishing the stone. Blemishes such as scratches and abrasions are sometimes considered as part of the finish grade of the stone. This book classifies them as clarity elements.

Judging the Face-up View

Colored stones should display maximum color. However, if they're cut with improper angles, their color potential can be diminished with what is called a **window**—a washed out area in the middle of the stone that allows you to see right through it. Windows (or windowing) can occur in any transparent, faceted stone no matter how light or dark it is and no matter how deep or shallow its pavilion. In general, the larger the window, the poorer the cut. Windowed stones are the attempt of the cutter to maximize weight at the expense of brilliance.

To look for windows, hold the stone about an inch or two (2 to 5 cm) above a contrasting background such as your hand or a piece of white paper. Then try to look straight through the top of the stone **without tilting it**, and check if you can see the background or a light window-like area in the center of it. If the stone is light colored, you might try holding it above a printed page to see if the print shows through. If the center area of the stone is pale or lifeless compared to a darker faceted area surrounding the pale center, this is also a window effect.

Fig. 6.1 Ametrine with a distracting window

Left: **Fig 6.2** Peridots with no window from Cynthia Renée Co. *Photo by Robert Weldon*

When evaluating a stone for windowing, you will probably notice dark areas in it. The GIA refers to these as **extinction areas** or simply **extinction**. All transparent faceted gems have some dark areas. However, a good cut can reduce extinction and increase color. One should expect dark stones to have a higher percentage of dark areas than those which are lighter colored. You should also expect there to be more extinction than what you see in pictures of gems. During shooting, photographers normally use two or more front lights to make stones show as much color as possible. When you look at a stone, you will usually be using a single light source, so less color and more black will show. The broader and more diffused the light is, the more colorful the stone will look. Therefore, compare stones under the same type and amount of lighting.

The quality, complexity and originality of the faceting should also be considered when judging cut. Some of the best faceting is done on low- and medium-priced gem material such as topaz aquamarine, garnet, quartz, tanzanite and tourmaline. The faceting and proportioning of more expensive stones like emeralds and rubies is often less precise because the higher cost of the rough leads many cutters to be more interested in retaining weight than in maximizing beauty. Finding an emerald or ruby without windowing can be difficult. Nevertheless, emeralds, rubies and other expensive stones can be well-cut and display good color and brilliance. For more photos and information on faceting styles, see Chapter 2.

When you hear the term **brilliance** used, keep in mind that it has different definitions. In the GIA Colored Stone Grading Course, it is defined as the percentage of light return in a gem after the percentage of windowing and extinction are subtracted. AGL (American Gemological Laboratories) uses "brilliance" only in connection with the amount of windowing present. A stone with no window whatsoever would receive a brilliance grade of 100%. This high of a brilliance percentage would not be possible under the GIA system because there is always some extinction present in transparent faceted gems. In this book, the term "brilliant" is used in the colloquial sense of having both a high intensity and large area of light return. A dull-looking, low-transparency stone with no window would not be described as "brilliant" under this non-technical definition.

Another thing to notice when judging the face-up view of a gem is the outline of the shape. If it's a standard shape that should be symmetrical, check to see if it is. If you plan to resell the stone later, make sure it's a shape others might like. A very long, skinny marquise or emerald cut, for example, may be hard to sell. With stones such as ruby, emerald and alexandrite, conserving weight from the rough is often more of a priority than good symmetry.

Fig. 6.3 A yellow-orange sapphire with no window and a good play of light and color off the facets

Fig. 6.4 Side view of same stone. Sapphires with good brilliance are typically deeper than diamonds. This stone is a little deep for some mountings.

Judging the Profile

When you buy a gemstone, be sure to look at its profile. The side view can indicate:

♦ If the stone is suitable for mounting in jewelry.

♦ If the stone will look big or small for its weight.

♦ If the cutter's main goal was to bring out the stone's brilliance.

When evaluating the profile, hold the stone with the shortest side facing you (widthwise) and **check the overall depth** (referred to in the trade as the **total depth percentage**). If you look at it lengthwise, the stone could look too shallow when in fact it may have an adequate depth. You should expect well-cut colored stones to be deeper than diamonds, which have a high refractive index (a measure of the degree to which light is bent as it travels through a gem).

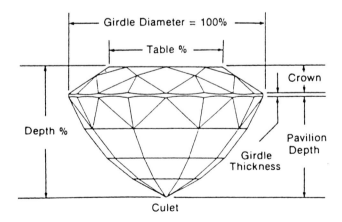

Fig. 6.5 Profile diagram of a mixed-cut colored stone. *Copyright 1978 by American Gemological Laboratories, Inc.*

Noted mineralogist John Sinkankas makes this point in his book, *Emerald and Other Beryls* (page 334): "In the case of higher refractive index gemstones, inner reflections can result from

Fig. 6.6 Profile of an amethyst with a pavilion that is so shallow it creates a large window

Left: **Fig. 6.7** Face up view of the amethyst in fig. 6.6. Note the extremely large window.

shallower bottom angles, thus allowing these gems to be cut less deeply. This becomes apparent when two brilliant gems of the same size and style of cutting are compared, one being diamond and the other a beryl. It will be seen that the diamond is cut to less depth while the beryl had to be cut to greater depth in order to insure upward reflection of light."

The **total depth percentage** of the stone in the profile diagram of figure 6.5 can be calculated as follows: **depth**
        width (girdle diameter)

In this case, the total depth percentage is 65%, which is a good depth/width ratio for a colored stone. There are differences of opinion as to which is the best depth percentage for a colored stone cut in a traditional style such as an emerald cut or round brilliant cut. Some say 60 to 65%. Others say 65 to 80%. Combining these two ranges, we can conclude that a stone's depth should range between 60 to 80% of its width.

If a stone is too deep, it may not be suitable for mounting in jewelry and it will look small for its weight in the face-up view. The main reason for cutting extremely deep stones is to save as much weight from the original rough as possible. Stones may also be cut deep to darken their color, especially if they are pale or color-zoned. Unnecessary weight adds to the cost of the stone since prices are calculated by multiplying the weight times the per-carat cost. Consequently, when you compare the prices of stones, you should consider their overall depth.

If a stone is extremely shallow ("flat") when you look at it widthwise, it might be fragile and therefore unsuitable as a stone for an everyday ring (it could, however, be good for a pendant, brooch or earrings). Very shallow stones look big for their weight in the face-up view, but unfortunately they often have big windows and lack life, which brings down their value (figs.6.6 & 6.7). The main reason for cutting extremely shallow stones is to maintain the shape of the original rough so as not to lose too much weight. Stones may also be cut shallow to lighten their color. Some cutters are able to take flat gem rough and cut it into attractive, brilliant stones using non-traditional cutting styles (figs 6.8 & 6.10). The Torus Ring™ is an example of this. It faces up larger than a normal stone of the same weight without any sacrifice to brilliance. In this case, the total depth percentage of the gemstone is irrelevant. What matters is the overall appearance.

When judging the profile of a gemstone, you should also pay attention to the **crown height and the pavilion depth.** Notice the relationship of the crown height to the pavilion depth in the profile diagram of figure 6.5 (about 3.5 to 1). Then compare the profile views in this chapter to the diagram. Without even measuring these stones, you can make visual judgments about their pavilion and crown heights.

Fig. 6.8 Amethyst, citrine, peridot & garnet torus rings™ carved by Glenn Lehrer. These are examples of how a skilled, imaginative cutter can bring out brilliance, yet minimize weight loss in flat rough. *Photo by Azad.*

If the **crown** is too low, the stone will lack sparkle. When light falls on a thin crown, there tends to be a large sheet-like reflection off the table facet instead of twinkles of light from the other crown facets. Some cutters intentionally cut stones with no crowns in order to draw your eye into the interior of the stone. This is commonly seen in fantasy-style cuts. These stones should be judged on their general appearance, not according to traditional standards.

Fig. 6.9 A tanzanite with a thin crown

If the **pavilion** is too flat or too deep, the stone may lack life, have a window, or look blackish. In order for the stone to effectively reflect light, the pavilion and crown must be angled properly. But they can't have the proper angles if they don't have the proper depth.

While evaluating the profile, look at the curvature of the pavilion outline. A lumpy, bulging pavilion decreases brilliance and helps create dark or window-like areas in the stone. This is because the pavilion is not slanted at an angle that will maximize light reflection. A bulging pavilion is not uncommon in expensive stones. Its another example of how you can end up paying for excess weight that reduces the beauty of the stone. Unlike diamonds, colored stones should have a slight pavilion curvature. This helps decrease windowing as the stone is tilted.

Notice, too, the **symmetry** of the profile. Symmetry problems such as an **off-center culet** prevent light from reflecting evenly. (In cushions, ovals and marquises, the culet should be centered widthwise and lengthwise. In hearts and pear-shapes, the culet should be placed at the widest portion of the stone.) It's common for rubies, emeralds, sapphires and alexandrites to look less symmetrical than stones such as diamonds. However, when stones are so lopsided that their brilliance is seriously diminished, the lack of symmetry is unacceptable.

Fig. 6.10 These concave-faceted citrines and amethyst have excellent brilliance and no window. They were cut by Mark Gronlund. Even though their proportions may not meet traditional standards, they're well cut.

Also check the **girdle width**. Stones with very thin girdles are difficult to set and easy to chip. Stones with thick girdles have reduced brilliance, look smaller than they weigh, and are also difficult to set. The judgment of girdle thickness is best done with the eye, with and without magnification. If the girdle looks like a wide band encircling the stone, it's probably too thick. If the girdle is sharp and you can hardly see it, then it's probably too thin. **Wavy and uneven girdles** can also create setting problems. In addition, they indicate that the cutter did not pay much attention to detail.

How Cut Affects Price

Theoretically, cutting defects should reduce gem prices. In actual practice, this isn't always true.

Sometimes the cut may have no direct effect on the per-carat price. For example a 1/2-carat sapphire pendant may be mass-produced and sold at the same price in chain stores. Some of the sapphires may be well-cut. Others of similar color and clarity may have large windows. In spite of their identical price, the value of the better-cut sapphires should be greater.

In some stores, you can select a gem from an assortment of stones in a packet or little bowl. The per-carat price for all the stones may be the same even though they might vary in quality. People who know how to evaluate gems will get the best buys in cases like these because they will be able to pick out the most valuable stones and avoid paying for unnecessary weight.

Sometimes the cut has a mathematically calculated effect on the price of gems. For example, the prices of fine-quality princess cuts that are calibrated to specific millimeter sizes may be determined by the weight lost when cutting the stones.

If you were to have a large stone recut to bring out its brilliance, you could calculate its new per-carat price by dividing the new weight into the combined cost of the recutting and the stone. The increased value of a stone after recutting can more than make up for its lost weight and cutting costs. Consequently, it is not uncommon for fine-quality gem material to be recut to improve the proportions. There are risks, however, to recutting gems—breakage or color lightening..

Sometimes the cut affects prices in a subjective manner. Some dealers place a greater importance on cut than others, and they may discount a very poorly cut stone as much as 50% in order to sell it. Another dealer might discount the same stone 25%. Premiums of between 10 to 25% may be added to precision-cut stones. But considering the fact that fine-cut stones don't have unnecessary weight, their total cost may not be much more than that of a bulky stone with the same face-up size.

There is no established trade formula for determining percentage-wise how cut affects the value of gems. There is, however, agreement that a well-proportioned, brilliant stone is more valuable than one which is poorly cut. As you shop, you may discover that well-cut stones are not always readily available, particularly in the case of emeralds and rubies. This is unfortunate because man has control over a stone's cut. Cutting has improved over the last ten years because of demands from customers. Achieving brilliance is becoming more important than saving weight. If this trend continues, it will be easier for you to find well-cut gems.

Judging "Life"

The term "life" is frequently used by dealers to refer to the overall brilliance and sparkle of a gem. Some people equate it to "cut," but it's different because a stone can be well-cut yet have poor life. Even though it is one of the most important value factors, "life" is not listed as a grading category on gem lab reports or appraisals—probably because it's difficult to define and quantify. It's subjective. Some of the factors that can influence your impression of "life" are:

Transparency. The higher the transparency, the greater the life. This is a key factor in determining life in stones such as ruby and emerald, which due to inclusions, tend to have a lower transparency than most other "transparent gems".

Faceting style. Brilliant- and mixed-cut stones generally have more life than step cuts. Step-cut stones, such as emerald cuts, can look lively, but ones expectation of life in those stones should be lower. Stones with concave facets may display greater brilliance than those with flat facets.

Proportions. Well-proportioned stones will return more light to the eye than poorly cut stones with windows. A gem can be well proportioned, though, and still lack life.

Polish. The higher the polish, the brighter a gem will look. Hard stones can take a higher polish than softer stones, so there are different expectations of polish luster depending on the gem species.

Clarity. Inclusions can impede light and brilliance, thereby lowering the life of a gem.

Amount of gray present. Often the more grayish a stone is the duller it looks. This is one of the reasons grayish stones tend to be less valued than stones with purer colors. Even gray diamonds can look dull, which is probably why at the wholesale level, they may cost less than yellowish diamonds of the same tone.

Tone. The lighter a stone is the more brilliant it can be. Keep in mind, though, that deep, saturated colors are much more highly valued than light colors.

Sometimes we get so involved in analyzing the color, clarity and cut of gems that we forget to notice if they have "life." As you browse in jewelry stores, make a special effort to notice the overall brilliance of the gems. This helps develop the eye. Once you can recognize a fine-cut, lively stone, you'll be well on your way to spotting value.

7

Star & Cat's-Eye Stones

C abochons (gems with a domed, polished surface) can resemble a cat's eye when they have many needle-like inclusions or hollow tubes, all parallel to each other, and are cut properly. When the cabochon is placed under a concentrated light source such as a light bulb, a band of reflected light is visible across the top of the cabochon. This effect is called **chatoyancy**, and stones that display it are said to be **chatoyant**. *(Chat* means "cat" in French.)

The term "cat's-eye" when used by itself also refers to the chatoyant variety of chrysoberyl, a gem species. Other minerals such as beryl, quartz, tourmaline and zircon can also display a cat's-eye, but these stones must include the mineral name—for example, "cat's-eye quartz" or "quartz cat's-eye." Besides the cat's-eye effect, these stones may show what is called the "**milk and honey effect**" (fig. 7.2)—when the stone is held with the eye at a right angle to a beam of light, the half of the stone nearest the light shows the body color of the stone, while the other half looks milky. When the stone is rotated between two lights, the chatoyant band appears to open and close. The open position is shown in figure 7.4.

Top-quality cat's-eye stones have the following characteristics:

♦ They have a sharp, straight, narrow band (eye) positioned in the center of the cabochon. The band is distinct and not too thin.
♦ The band of reflected light is white or gray, not the same color hue as the stone's background.
♦ The eye extends all the way across the stone.
♦ The stone has no distracting flaws.
♦ The stone is neither opaque or transparent.

Unfortunately, there aren't many stones that meet all these criteria. When buying gemstones it's often necessary to compromise on some quality factors. Don't expect cat's-eye stones to be free of eye-visible flaws or to have perfect symmetry. Don't worry if a little of the stone's color shows through in the eye. The most important consideration when buying a chatoyant gem is that it has a distinct eye.

The needle inclusions in cat's-eye stones line up in one direction like thread on a spool; but in some gems they align themselves in groups oriented in different directions. When these stones are cut as cabochons, the bands of reflected light may cross each other in the center, creating a star. This effect is called **asterism**. The half of a band that starts from the center of the stone and goes to the edge is called a **ray**. Star gems generally have from four to twelve rays. Star rubies and star sapphires are the best known star gems. Other gems that can display a star include beryl, garnet, quartz and spinel.

Fig. 7.1 Cat's-eye. *Photo and ring from Hubert Inc.*

Fig. 7.2 Milk and honey effect **Fig. 7.3** Cat's-eye **Fig. 7.4** Opening and closing effect

In 1947, synthetic star ruby and sapphire stones were introduced to the market by the Linde Division of the Union Carbide Corporation in the United States. They were an instant success, and ever since that time there has been a tendency to expect natural stones to resemble them. It's true that there are some very fine deep blue and red specimens in museums and private collections, but these are the exception rather than the rule. Most natural star sapphires are normally more pale than natural faceted sapphires, and their stars are not as well defined as those of laboratory-grown (synthetic) stones. Star rubies often have a maroon rather than red color and their stars tend to be indistinct and imperfect.

Even though lab-grown star sapphires and rubies usually have sharper stars and a more intense color than a natural stone, they are not highly valued. They can be found in jewelry supply stores for between $10 and $50 per stone. (However, some of the newer synthetic stones with lighter colors and more natural looking stars sell for a lot more.) In contrast, a natural stone with a similar color and size but a less perfect star than a $30 synthetic stone could sell for several thousand dollars.

Your main concern when judging a star stone should be: is it easy to see the star when you look at the stone under a single, direct light source such as a penlight or light-bulb? (The star will hardly be noticeable in diffuse light from fluorescent lights or overcast skies.) Some secondary questions to ask are:

Fig. 7.5 Star sapphire (6.80 cts). It's unusual to find a natural blue star sapphire with such a distinct and well-centered star. *Photo from Asian Institute of Gemological Sciences (AIGS)*

- Is the star centered?
- Is the star sharp and well defined?
- Are the rays straight?
- Are all the rays present?
- Do the rays extend completely across the stone?
- Is there a good contrast between the star and the background?

57

Fig. 7.6 A low-priced Indian star ruby with an irregular star

Fig. 7.7 A more expensive star ruby. Note the sharper star.

Fig. 7.8 Synthetic star sapphire. Note how long and sharp the rays are.

Ideally you should be able to answer yes to all of the preceding questions. In actuality, however, the stars on natural stones tend to be slightly wavy, a little blurry and/or incomplete. Quite often the better the color is, the more imperfect the star looks. Appraisers normally indicate the degree to which the stars conform to the above standards. Under the category of star centering, for example, they may indicate poor, fair, good, very good or excellent.

The degree of transparency also plays a major role in determining the value of star gems. As a general rule, the more transparent a star stone is, the greater its value. A translucent Indian star ruby, for example, may sell for ten times more than if it were opaque.

The evaluation of color in star stones is similar to that of faceted stones, but the overall grading is more lenient. Generally, the more saturated and pure the body color, the more valuable the stone is. Medium and medium-dark tones tend to be the most prized. Light tones, however, are considered acceptable. Natural star sapphires other than the black variety tend to be light blue or gray.

It's normal for star stones to have flaws. However, the more obvious these flaws are to the naked eye, the lower the value of the stone. It's usually best to avoid stones with a lot of surface cracks because they may not be very durable, and they may be dyed.

Star gems have often been worn as good-luck charms. In his book, *The Curious Lore of Precious Stones,* George Kunz states that the three cross-bars of the star were thought to represent faith, hope and destiny. Supposedly, star sapphires were so powerful at warding off bad omens that they would exercise their good influence over their first owners even after passing into other hands. Even today, star stones are worn for good luck, and they are still available. However, don't expect natural star stones to have perfect clarity, symmetry and stars. To find a stone that meets these criteria, consider buying a synthetic stone.

8

Treatments

I f the supply of gems were limited to those specimens that are naturally attractive, they'd be so expensive that most of us could never own them. Therefore, many gems are treated. A **treatment** is any process such as heating, oiling, irradiation, waxing, dying or bleaching which alters the color or clarity of a gem.

Enhancement is often used as another word for treatment. However, it has a broader meaning. "Enhancement" also refers to the faceting and polishing of a gem. In addition, it sounds more positive, which can lead buyers to believe that treatments are always beneficial when they aren't. If stones are improperly heated, for example, they may become brittle, causing them to abrade more easily. Some treatments are not stable. To avoid any misunderstandings, this book normally uses the term "treatment."

In Europe, some gem labs use the term "enhancement" on their reports to refer to routine treatments that are well accepted on colored gems. "Treatment" is reserved for unaccepted treatments. This policy has the effect of turning "treatment" into a negative term when in fact it's a neutral term by dictionary definition. A treatment can be good or bad; it depends on the type of treatment and how it's done. It makes more sense to simply state on lab reports the type of treatment a stone has undergone. The buyer can then determine if it's acceptable or not.

"Treatment" is the standard term used in gemological literature and at conferences for any process done to improve the appearance of a gemstone, except for cutting and cleaning. If we try to avoid or ban its use with the general public, it could give the impression that the trade doesn't believe in full disclosure of treatments.

Gem Treatments

HEAT TREATMENT: For centuries, gems have been heated to improve their color. However, in the past 30 years, heat treatment has been conducted on a wider scale and at much higher temperatures—1600°C (2900°F) and above. Besides lightening or darkening the color of a stone, heat can improve its clarity. Unless a receipt or lab document states otherwise, you should assume that the following gemstones have probably been heat-treated: aquamarine, carnelian, ruby, sapphire, tanzanite, pink topaz, green tourmaline and blue zircon.

Heat treating is widely accepted because it's a continuation of a natural process and it causes a permanent improvement of the entire stone. From the standpoint of value, it doesn't matter whether commercial-quality stones have been treated or not as long as the color is permanent. The overall quality of the treated stone determines the price. However, a premium may be charged for high-quality *untreated* stones that come with a lab report stating there is no evidence of heat treatment.

If heat treatment is not handled properly, stones may become brittle and therefore less durable. When buying a ruby or a sapphire check to see if the stone has severe abrasions and pits. Because of their hardness, such stones should normally provide good wear. However, if the stone you're considering has never been worn and most of the facet edges are abraded, it might have a durability problem caused by improper heating.

IRRADIATION: Various types of radiation are used to intensify or change the color of certain gems. Gamma rays from a cobalt or cesium source are the preferred irradiation agent because they don't induce radioactivity. Pink tourmaline is one example of a stone that is commonly treated with gamma radiation to intensify its color. Untreated pink and red tourmaline owe their color to natural radiation. The gamma treatment speeds up the natural process of making colorless tourmaline pink or red. The strength of the color can be a measure of the dose of radiation the stone received naturally and/or through treatment. The color is relatively stable, but strong heat from lights, for example, may sometimes cause it to fade. Fortunately, irradiation treatment will bring back the color. Irradiated pink and red tourmalines are free of radioactivity because the gamma treatment does not change the nuclei of their atoms. Instead, some of the outer electrons are moved to different positions, creating what are called *color centers* which change the way the stone absorbs light.

Topaz is another example of a stone that is routinely irradiated. But in order to obtain the desirable intense blue color, the irradiation is done by one of three different processes. In most cases, colorless topaz is irradiated in a high-energy electron-beam linear accelerator and/or nuclear reactor, which usually turns it brown. The topaz is then heat-treated to produce the stable blue color. The irradiation uses much higher energy levels than that for red tourmaline. This can result in a change to the nucleus of the atoms of impurities in the topaz, creating radioactivity. It may take a few days to many years for the radioactivity to decay. There have been a few isolated cases where blue topaz was sold before it was safe, particularly in the 1980's. In many countries, treated gems are now regulated and must meet certain standards. The United States has the strictest requirements. When suppliers of blue topaz guarantee that their stones come from a licensed facility that's in compliance with standards set by the Nuclear Regulatory Commission, you need not worry about radioactivity in topaz.

Only certain other gem varieties can be enhanced with irradiation. They include:

Maxixe- (ma SHE she) **type beryl**—dark blue beryl from pale pink or colorless beryl; fades.
Yellow beryl—from colorless beryl; some fades in light or heat.
Smoky quartz—from colorless quartz (rock crystal); stable.
Yellow or orange sapphire—from colorless and light yellow sapphire; fades in minutes to days
   Most yellow sapphire is heat treated, not irradiated.
Diamonds that are green, blue, yellow or brown—from light yellow or brown diamond; stable.
"Black" or **Dark-Color Pearls**—from off-color bleached pearls; stable, after a slight fading just
   after treatment.

The information on radiation treatment in this section comes primarily from the book *Gemstone Enhancement* by Dr. Kurt Nassau and from personal communication with Dr. Horst Krupp and Dr. Nassau, both physicists, mineralogists and gemologists.

FRACTURE FILLING & FRACTURE HEALING: When surface-reaching fractures in gems are filled with an appropriate substance, they are less noticeable and the overall color and transparency may improve. Emeralds typically have small surface-reaching cracks so they're commonly filled with oil, wax or an epoxy-type substance. Unfortunately, the filling can evaporate and may sometimes leave a white or brown residue. This is not a major problem if the stone has been oiled because the stone can be cleaned out by repeated immersion in a solvent such as lacquer thinner. Afterwards it can be re-oiled to look as good as when bought. Some hardened epoxies, however, may be difficult to extract. Therefore fillers which are easy to remove and as stable as possible tend to be the preferred types of fillers for emerald.

Ruby is another stone that may be oiled or filled with epoxy when surface-reaching cracks are present. However, unlike emerald oiling, ruby oiling is not accepted by the trade.

Glass-like fillings may also be present in some rubies. During heat treatment, a borax solution used on the stones can melt and form a glass that seeps into fractures and cavities. This improves the stones' appearance. This process is often referred to as infilling or fracture-healing. It's less accepted than heat treatment but more accepted than ruby oiling because it's relatively permanent and irreversible. It may also improve a stone's durability since the fractures are healed shut.

The extent of the filling treatment should be a consideration when buying expensive stones. Gem labs now indicate on their documents the extent of the filling process, often by describing it as minor, moderate, significant or none. The less filler present the more desirable the gem. For more information on fracture filling and other treatments consult the *Ruby, Sapphire & Emerald Buying Guide* by Renée Newman.

DYEING (STAINING): Rubies, emeralds, jade and other stones that may have small surface cracks are occasionally dyed with colored oils, epoxies or dyes, especially if they are of very low quality. Some gemstones like lapis lazuli, chalcedony and agate don't need surface cracks to accept dye. They are naturally porous and often dyed. Black onyx is just dyed chalcedony.

Dyed lapis and dyed chalcedony are accepted in the trade, but dyed rubies, emeralds and jade are not. There's nothing wrong with dyed stones as long as you're informed that they're treated and told how to care for them. Dye treatments provide a practical means of making low-grade stones look better. Unfortunately, these stones are often sold with the intent of fooling buyers. Then, instead of being a legitimate treatment, dyeing becomes a deceptive practice.

SURFACE DIFFUSION (BULK DIFFUSION): This treatment is most often done on sapphires, rubies or topaz to turn pale or colorless stones blue, orange, yellow, red or green. It may also be used to form a star. Coloring agents like titanium, chromium, and beryllium are diffused into the stone to change its color. For example, pale stones may be packed in chemical powders which impart color and then heated to 1700°C and above until a thin layer of color covers their surface or they may be heat treated with a material like chrysoberyl.

Fig. 8.1 Diffusion-treated green topaz & coated "Mystic Topaz." The white specks are areas where the coating has worn away

Surface diffusion is relatively new (about 30 years old, according to patent records) and is not yet very well accepted by the trade. However, it's becoming more prevalent. In 2002, gem labs discovered that much of the orange sapphire being released on the market was diffusion-treated Green topaz is becoming more common; it's also diffusion-treated (fig 8.1). The color is permanent, but often remains only on the surface of the stone. Consequently, the color can be polished or scraped off, leaving the grey or white interior exposed. In some cases the coloring agents may be deeply diffused. Some people sell diffusion-treated stones openly, but others try to pass them off as nontreated. Therefore when buying rubies and sapphires, ask if they have been diffusion treated. As for topaz, it doesn't occur naturally in emerald-green colors, so assume that deep green topaz has undergone a diffusion coloring process.

IMPREGNATION & COATING with wax plastic & iridescent substances: The ancient Romans used to wax their marble statues to hide cracks and to make the surface look shiny. Today gems are waxed and plasticized for the same reasons. Impregnation can also improve durability and color. Some of the stones that undergo this treatment are turquoise, jade, lapis, malachite, amazonite and topaz.

One coated stone that was recently introduced to the market is "**mystic topaz.**" It has a colorplay of green/purple or red/yellow which is the result of a special coating. It retails for about $10 per carat. Wear "mystic topaz" in pendants, pins and earrings, but not in rings because the coating can wear away if the stone is subjected to knocks or scrapes.

The treating of gemstones is one of the most controversial subjects in the gem trade. Most gem and jewelry organizations now encourage their members to disclose treatments; unfortunately, suppliers don't always tell jewelers how their stones have been treated, so retailers may not have adequate information to pass on to customers. Furthermore, detecting or identifying treatments is not easy. Even the world's foremost gem laboratories find this difficult and sometimes impossible. Nevertheless, jewelers and salespeople should be able to give you general information about gem treatments. For example, they should know that emeralds are usually treated with oil or other fillers to improve their clarity, and they should tell you this. They should also be able to explain to you why emeralds need special attention and how you should care for them. In most cases, however, it's not possible for sellers to know what kind of filler was used and to what extent the filling changed the clarity of the stone. To get more detailed information about a specific stone, you normally have to send it to a gem laboratory. This is advisable if you're buying an expensive gem.

If you don't know a salesperson, it's hard for you to tell if he or she is knowledgeable and ethical. One way of learning something about the character of sellers is to ask what kinds of treatments their stones have undergone. If they're candid and informed, this is a good sign. Reputable salespeople give their customers practical advice and basic facts about gem treatments.

Two excellent books for more in-depth information on treatments are:
Gemstone Enhancement, Second Edition by Kurt Nassau, Butterworth-Heinemann
Synthetic, Imitation & Treated Gemstones by Michael O'Donoghue, Butterworth-Heinemann

Other good sources are:
Australian Gemmologist. Gemmological Association of Australia, Brisbane
Gems and Gemology. Gemological Institute of America, Carlsbad, CA
Journal of Gemmology. Gemmological Association and Gem Testing Laboratory of Great Britain, London

9

Synthetic Stones

To the average person on the street, a synthetic is a fake. In the jewelry trade, though, the word **synthetic** is used differently. It describes a gemstone made in a lab which has the same basic chemical composition and similar chemical, optical and physical properties to its natural counterpart. **A natural gemstone** comes from the ground and is a product of nature, not of man. **Imitations**, on the other hand, do not have the same chemical composition as the stones they resemble, and they may be made by nature or by man. Red glass, for example, can be a man-made imitation of ruby. Garnets used to mimic rubies would be natural imitations.

Since consumers tend to interpret the word "synthetic" differently than jewelers, people who sell synthetic stones usually prefer to describe them with terms such as **created, lab-grown** or **man-made**. Gemologists and natural stone dealers usually identify lab-grown stones as synthetics.

Cultured is sometimes used as a synonym for "lab-grown." The two terms, however, are not equivalent. Culturing pearls is a more natural process than growing gems. A cultured pearl has a nacre coating that is grown in a natural organism and secreted by a natural organism. Man just inserts the irritant into the mollusk. On the other hand, created gems are grown in a lab, not in a natural environment such as the ground, and the chemical ingredients are supplied by man, not by nature through a natural process.

Synthetic gems are not just a recent phenomenon. Lab-grown ruby, the first synthetic, has been sold commercially since the early 1900's; if your grandmother has some ruby jewelry, the stones could very well have been made in a laboratory. Today, lab-grown stones are even more common, especially in birthstone jewelry and class rings. Synthetics are also found in designer jewelry, set with diamonds in gold or platinum. Some of the stones that are synthetically produced and sold to consumers in jewelry are:

Synthetic alexandrite	Synthetic citrine	Synthetic opal
Synthetic amethyst	Synthetic diamond	Synthetic ruby
Synthetic aquamarine	Synthetic emerald	Synthetic sapphire
Synthetic beryl (red, yellow)	Synthetic garnet	Synthetic spinel
Synthetic chrysoberyl	Synthetic lapis lazuli	Synthetic turquoise

Some stores call imitation stones "synthetic." For example, imitation tanzanite may be sold as "synthetic tanzanite" because "synthetic" sounds better than "imitation." Green CZ (cubic zirconia) is often called synthetic emerald. Green CZ is a lab-grown stone, but it's not synthetic emerald. It's synthetic CZ, which is much cheaper than lab-grown emerald. The retail price difference between the two stones can be over $150 per carat.

According to the guidelines of the United States Federal Trade Commission (FTC), "(c) It is unfair or deceptive to use the word "laboratory-grown," "laboratory-created" "(manufacturer name)-

created," or "synthetic" with the name of any natural stone to describe any industry product unless such industry product has essentially the same optical, physical, and chemical properties as the stone named."

Synthetic Versus Natural

Both natural and synthetic stones of the same gem variety have essentially the same chemical composition, hardness, luster and refractive qualities. However, there will be some important commercial differences, namely:

Price: Most lab-grown stones cost much less than their natural counterparts. The price is determined by their availability, the process used to grow them and market competition.

When lab-grown ruby first appeared on the market, it cost about as much as natural ruby. Today you can buy the same type of lab-grown ruby for less than a couple of dollars a carat. When well-cut, it can be quite attractive. Some synthetic rubies which are grown by a different process may retail for over $300 per carat. This is still much less than if they were natural and had the same color and clarity.

Appearance: One of the biggest advantages of lab-grown stones is that they look attractive and expensive, yet they are normally a lot more affordable than high-quality natural stones.

Rarity: Lab-grown stones can be produced in whatever quantities are needed. As a result, they are readily available. High quality natural stones may be rare and therefore valuable. Finding a good-quality natural stone in the size or shape you'd like is often difficult. You may have to compromise on size, quality, or color.

Emotional Value: Natural gemstones have traditionally had an aura of mystery due to their long, intriguing history and the remote places in which they are mined. Consumers interested in the romantic aspects of gems will generally attach a greater emotional value to a natural stone than one created quickly in a laboratory. To them, there may be no substitute for the "real thing."

Potential for Price Appreciation: Despite market fluctuations, the overall value of natural gems has usually increased over the years. As a result, some have been accepted as a medium of exchange and as collateral for loans. Created gems have not enjoyed this prestige. Instead, their price has generally gone down as production and competition have increased. Rather than being viewed as a portable treasure, synthetic stones are considered an affordable alternative to the natural stone.

Some people may ask, "Why did scientists have to complicate the gem business by creating synthetics?" It's true that synthetic stones have been used to deceive people, and the process of identification has become more complicated. But there's a positive side, too. Thanks to lab-grown stones, people who can't afford certain natural gems are still able to own stones such as good-quality, synthetic rubies and emeralds. Synthetic gem material also benefits industry by being used in lasers, machinery, jets, communication devices, etc. In fact, it's industrial needs that spurred research into the development of synthetic gems.

The next time you admire an attractive gem that's beyond your budget, ask if it's available as a synthetic. If it is, this may be a good option for you. Your friends probably won't know the difference; they'll just compliment you on your good taste in gems and wonder how you could afford them.

10

Deceptive Practices

There is no fraud or deceit in the world which yields greater gain and profit than that of counterfeiting gems. (Pliny the Elder, Roman scholar, from his 37th Book of the Historie of the World, 1st century AD)

Unfortunately, the counterfeiting of gems is as widespread as ever. Today, there are just more ways of doing it. In Pliny's day, there were no lab-grown gemstones. Irradiation and diffusion treatments were unknown. There's nothing wrong with creating synthetics or treating gems. Fraud occurs when a customer is not told that his stone is synthetic or treated.

Listed below are practices that are normally done with the intent to deceive. All of them, however, can be considered legitimate when they are properly disclosed to buyers.

COATING with colored substances: Colorless or pale colored stones are sometimes coated with colored plastic. Green plastic coatings are used to make colorless beryl look like emerald and light green jade like valuable imperial jade. Rock crystal coated with red plastic resembles ruby. Occasionally, transparent metallic coatings, like those on modern camera lenses, are applied to colorless gems to add color or brilliance. Varnish and lacquer coatings may also be used. One noteworthy case occurred in 1983 when a 9.58-carat diamond was put up for sale at a major auction in New York. It was supposed to be a fancy pink diamond valued at $500,000. Someone managed to switch it with a light yellow diamond coated with pink nail polish that was worth about one fourth of the appraised value. The deception was discovered a day before the sale.

PAINTING: You don't have to cover a pale stone with a colored coating to make it look colorful. A little paint in the right spot(s) can do the job. Due to the multiple reflections in a faceted transparent gem, a dab or two of paint on the bottom and/or edge of the stone can make it appear evenly colored when viewed face up. The paint can be hidden by the mounting. Emeralds have at times been colored in this manner. Translucent opal cabochons may be painted on the bottom to enhance and intensify their play of color. Peacock feathers, multi-colored butterfly wings and mother of pearl have on occasion been placed behind opal to improve color play too. Sometimes purple ink is applied on the back of yellowish diamonds or under the prongs of the setting to make the diamonds appear almost colorless and more valuable. Since purple is the complimentary color of yellow, it has the effect of absorbing part of the yellow color. As a result, **beware of closed-back settings**. The bottom of the stone may be painted.

FOIL BACKING: For probably 4000 years, foil backings have been used to add color and brilliance to gems. As gem-cutting techniques progressed and brought out more brilliance in stones, these backings became less popular. Today foil backings are occasionally found on genuine stones, but they are more likely to be seen on glass imitations. Again, **beware of closed-back settings**. Something such as foil may be concealed underneath the stones, particularly if they are unusually bright. Foil-backed stones are commonly found in antique pieces. The price of this jewelry should be based on its antique value.

QUENCH CRACKLING: Stones that are quench crackled have been heated and then plunged into cold water. This procedure is done to produce cracks in synthetic stones so they'll look more natural. Sometimes oil or other liquids are forced into the cracks to imitate the fingerprint inclusions found in natural gems. Colorless quartz may be quench crackled so it can afterwards be fracture-filled with colored oil or dyes and used to imitate emerald or ruby.

COMPOSITE STONES (ASSEMBLED STONES): Stones formed from two or more parts are called **composite** or **assembled stones**. If they're composed of two parts, they're **doublets**. Those consisting of three parts are **triplets**. Assembled opals are one of the most typical composite stones. Opal doublets and triplets are normally disclosed and sold in a legitimate manner so selling them is **not** considered a deceptive practice. Sapphire and ruby doublets, however, are generally used to trick buyers.

Listed below are various types of assembled stones that are sold on the market:

♦ **Natural stone + natural stone of the same gem species:** Natural stones may be glued together for a couple of reasons. One large stone (especially if it's over 1 carat) can be sold for a higher per carat price than two smaller ones. Also, composite stones may have a more valuable color than their individual parts. For example, pale yellow sapphire pieces may be cemented with a blue glue to form a blue sapphire, or opal with a play of color may be glued to common opal.

♦ **Natural stone + synthetic stone of the same gem species:** This is one of the most common types of composite stones. When examined under magnification, it may appear completely natural due to the presence of natural inclusions. The pavilion may be, for example, a deep blue synthetic sapphire, and the crown might consist of pale natural sapphire. The resulting stone is deep blue. Ruby doublets with a synthetic ruby pavilion and a thin natural sapphire crown are quite common.

♦ **Natural stone + glass or a different stone:** One of the best known composite stones is the garnet and glass doublet. It was invented in the mid 1800's to imitate gems of every color. It's a more suitable imitation than glass because the garnet crown is more durable and adds luster to the stone. If you own or have an interest in antique jewelry, you should be especially aware of these doublets. Many of the expensive-looking stones in antique pieces (especially those of the latter half of the 19th century) are nothing but garnet and glass doublets. Today garnet and glass doublets are rare. Glass has also been glued to other stones such as quartz and tanzanite. Slices of opal may be glued to glass, ironstone or black onyx.

♦ **Natural stone + colored glue or gelatin layer + same or another stone:** In Europe and the British Commonwealth countries, this type of assembled stone is called a doublet or **soudé stone** (French for "soldered stone)." In the United States, they're often called triplets. An emerald triplet in the U.S., for example, consists of two pieces of pale emerald that are joined together with a green gelatin or cement, which is considered to be the third layer. Jade triplets have also been made. They consist of pale jade that has been hollowed out, filled with a green gel and smaller cabochon and then cemented to a jade back to make it look like expensive green jade.

A thin slice of opal cemented with black glue to another material such as potch opal, chalcedony or glass can resemble black opal. This stone is called an **opal doublet**. If it also has a protective top of colorless quartz or glass, then it is called an **opal triplet**.

The key to identifying a composite stone is to find where its parts have been joined together. This can often be seen by immersing the stone in water (immersion tends to make color differences and the glue layer more obvious). Do not immerse assembled opals in water or other liquids; just look at them from the side. Magnification is another helpful identifying technique. It can reveal separation lines, flattened air bubbles between the parts or swirly areas where the stone has been brushed with glue.

Misnomers

Sometimes gems are sold under misleading names. For example, a garnet may be called an "American ruby" or "Cape ruby" to make it seem more valuable. If a salesperson adds a qualifying word or prefix to a gem name, ask him or her to explain what it means. Some misnomers are:

Japanese amethyst	synthetic amethyst
Oriental amethyst	purple sapphire
Ceylon diamond	zircon
Brazilian diamond	colorless topaz
Herkimer diamond	rock crystal quartz
Mogok diamond	topaz
Brazilian emerald	green tourmaline
Evening emerald	peridot
Indian emerald	dyed crackled quartz
Medina emerald	green glass
Oriental emerald	green sapphire
Spanish emerald	green glass
Soudé emerald	green composite stone
African jade	translucent green garnet
Amazon jade	amazonite feldspar
Australian jade	chrysoprase
Colorado jade	amazonite feldspar
Indian jade	aventurine quartz
Korea jade	serpentine
Pikes Peak jade	amazonite feldspar
Oregon jade	dark green jasper
Swiss jade	dyed chalcedony
German lapis	dyed blue jasper
Swiss lapis	dyed blue jasper
California moonstone	chalcedony

Black onyx	dyed chalcedony
Ceylon opal	moonstone
Slocum opal	an imitation opal
Balas ruby	spinel
Bohemian ruby	rose quartz
Brazilian ruby	topaz
California ruby	garnet
Cape ruby	garnet
Colorado ruby	garnet
Siberian ruby	tourmaline
Spinel ruby	spinel
Brazilian sapphire	tourmaline or topaz
Lux sapphire	iolite
Meru sapphire	tanzanite
Oriental sapphire	chrysoberyl
Spinel sapphire	spinel
Water sapphire	iolite
Topaz	sometimes erroneously used for citrine quartz
Oriental topaz	yellow sapphire
Madeira topaz	citrine quartz
Mystic topaz	a coated topaz
Smoky topaz	smoky quartz
Spanish topaz	citrine quartz

11

Gemstone Descriptions

T he *Gemstone Buying Guide* is designed to help you evaluate the quality of colored gems. That's why six of the preceding chapters were about gemstone value factors. This chapter will give you some brief information about the history, sources and characteristics of the most important gemstones on the market. Before we begin, here is some basic terminology you should know:

Gemstones often may be identified as a group, species or variety. A **group** is composed of a number of closely related species. "Garnet" is an example of a group name. A **species** name refers to a mineral with a characteristic crystal structure and chemical composition. Grossular is one of the species of the garnet group. Another example of a species is opal, but there is no opal group. A **variety** name is normally based on color, transparency or optical effects such as color changes and star patterns; but sometimes it has its origins in early history when chemical analyses and crystal structure determinations did not exist. Tsavorite is a green variety of grossular. Amethyst and rock crystal are varieties of quartz. They both have the same essential chemistry and crystal structure but differ in color.

Trade names are often given to gemstones. "Tsavorite" is a trade name that is shorter and more marketable than "transparent green grossular," which is technically a more correct term. **Misnomers** are names which do not correctly identify a gem. Two examples of misnomers are "Herkimer diamond" for colorless quartz and "Kashmir sapphire" when used for sapphire that is not from Kashmir (true Kashmir sapphires of high quality are sold at premium prices).

Sometimes people classify diamonds, rubies, sapphires and emeralds as **precious** gems and other stones such as garnet or opal as **semi-precious**. This is misleading. Some garnets and opals sell for several thousand dollars per carat. On the other hand, there are a lot of opaque rubies and sapphires that sell for less than $10 a carat. In certain contexts, "precious stone" may refer to any stone that is used as a gem. "Precious topaz" can mean real topaz as opposed to citrine quartz or it can refer to high-quality topaz. Since the terms "precious" and "semi-precious" are so confusing, many experts have recommended that they not be used to classify gems.

Each gem species has characteristics which distinguish it from other species. For easy reference, we'll list some of these characteristics below with their definitions.

Refractive Index (RI): the degree to which light is bent as it passes through the stone. This is measured with an instrument called a refractometer. Most colored gems have RI's that range between 1.43 and 1.98. Diamonds have an RI of approximately 2.42, which means they bend light about 2.42 times more than air does. This also means that light travels 2.42 times more slowly through diamonds than it does through air. As a general rule, the higher the RI is, the greater the potential brilliance of the stone. Other factors such as clarity, cut and color also affect brilliance. There can be some variation in the RI of a species depending on a stone's origin and color. This is due to the presence of impurities, which vary according to the source of the stone. The RI of a species may fall slightly above or below the RI ranges listed in this book.

Specific Gravity (SG): the ratio of a gem's density to the density of water. The higher the SG the greater the density is. The SG of most colored gemstones falls between 2.00 and 4.75.

Hardness: the resistance of a gem to scratching and abrasion. This can be classified using the Mohs scale of hardness. The Mohs scale rates the relative hardness of materials with numbers from 1 to 10. The 10 rating of a diamond is the highest and the 1 of talc is the lowest. The intervals between numbers on the scale are not equal, especially between 9 and 10. Ruby and sapphire rate a 9, but a diamond may be over 100 times harder. Some gems like diamond may even have a directional hardness where one direction or surface is harder than another.

Toughness: the resistance of a gem to breaking, chipping or cracking. This is a different property than hardness. Jade is a relatively soft gem material (6–7), yet it is the toughest.

Cleavage: the tendency for a mineral to split along crystal planes, where the atomic bonding is weak. A gemstone may have one or more directions of cleavage, which are classified as perfect (almost perfectly smooth), distinct or indistinct. Cleavage has a negative impact on toughness.

Crystal System: one of the seven classifications of the internal structure of a crystal. It is based on the symmetry of the crystal structure. The simplest and most symmetrical system is called isometric or cubic. The other six systems in the order of their decreasing symmetry are tetragonal, hexagonal, trigonal, orthorhombic, monoclinic and triclinic. For descriptions and diagrams of the seven crystal systems, consult *Gemstones of the World* by Walter Schumann. This book also provides information on stones not included in the *Gemstone Buying Guide.*

Materials which don't have a crystalline structure (e.g. glass) are called **amorphous.** Some gems such as jade and agate are a group of tiny crystals grown together. These gems are classified technically as aggregates (AGG) and are usually translucent to opaque.

Optic Character: the effect a gem material has on light. If it can split light into two rays, each travelling at different speeds, then it is **doubly refractive (DR).** If it does not polarize (split) light, the stone is **singly refractive (SR).** In a doubly refractive gem, there is either one or there are two directions in which light is not split as it passes through it. In other words, a DR stone will behave as if it is singly refractive in at least one direction. The directions of single refraction are called **optic axes.** If the stone has one direction of single refraction, it is **uniaxial**, if it has two, it is **biaxial**.

Doubly refractive gems will have two RI's if they are uniaxial and three RI's if they are biaxial. The numerical difference between the highest and lowest RI is called the **birefringence** or **birefraction.** When you look through stones with a high birefringence, such as peridot, zircon or calcite, the inclusions and facet edges will appear to be doubled. This book does not provide birefringence data, but it gives the optic sign (+ or -). If a uniaxial gem is positive, the lower RI is constant and the higher variable. A negative sign would indicate the reverse. If a biaxial gem is positive, the intermediate RI is closer to the low RI. If negative, it's closer to the high RI.

Pleochroism: the ability of certain gem materials to exhibit different colors when viewed from different directions under transmitted light. A ruby, for example, may appear purplish red in one direction and orangy-red in another. Since it can show two colors, it is **dichroic.** Stones like tanzanite, which can display three colors, are **trichroic.** The strength of pleochroism can range from very strong to very weak. In pastel and colorless stones, pleochroism may not be visible.

Much of the identification data on the following pages was taken from *Gems* by Robert Webster and the GIA *Gem Reference Guide.* Consult these two sources for further information.

Below is a chart which lists the first group of gems in this chapter in the order in which they are presented. It indicates if their name is a group, species or variety classification.

Group	Species	Varieties
Quartz	Crystallized quartz	Amethyst, ametrine, citrine, hawk's-eye, quartz cat's-eye, rock crystal, rose quartz, smoky quartz, tiger's-eye
Quartz	Cryptocrystalline / microcrystalline quartz (chalcedony)	Agate, bloodstone, carnelian, chalcedony, chrysocolla quartz, chrysoprase, jasper, onyx, plasma, sard
None	Chrysoberyl	Alexandrite, cat's-eye, yellow, green or brown (chrysoberyl)
Beryl	Beryl	Emerald, green beryl, aquamarine, Maxixe beryl, heliodor, morganite, goshenite, bixbite, cat's-eye beryl
Garnet	Andradite, spessartine, pyrope almandine, grossular	Demantoid, topazolite, melanite, rhodolite, hessonite, mali garnet, tsavorite, malaia garnet
None	Cordierite	Iolite
Pyroxene	Jadeite (jade)	Green, lavender, "red," gray or white (jadeite)
Amphibole	Actinolite/tremolite (jade)	Nephrite, green, black, brown or white (nephrite)
Sodalite	Lazurite	Lapis lazuli
None	Malachite	
Feldspar	Microcline, orthoclase, albite, oligoclase, labradorite	Moonstone, amazonite, sunstone
None	Opal	Common, white, black, boulder or fire (opal)
Olivine	Forsterite	Peridot, chrysolite
Pyroxene	Spodumene	Kunzite, hiddenite, green spodumene
None	Corundum	Ruby, sapphire, padparadscha, star ruby, star sapphire
Spinel	Spinel	Red, pink, orange, blue or star (spinel)
Epidote	Zoisite	Tanzanite, thulite, green zoisite
None	Topaz	Pink, red, yellow, orange, blue, green or colorless (topaz)
Tourmaline	Elbaite, dravite, chrome dravite, schorl	Green, pink, red, yellow, orange, blue, watermelon, colorless, cat's-eye, bi-color (tourmaline), indicolite
Turquoise	Turquoise	
None	Zircon	Blue, green, red, yellow, orange or brown (zircon)

Amethyst & Other Quartz Stones SiO_2—silica (crystallized quartz)

Amethyst—February birthstone and 6th wedding anniversary stone; Citrine—alternate birthstone for November and 13th wedding anniversary stone

Throughout history, supernatural powers have been ascribed to amethyst, rock crystal and other quartz stones. Amethyst, supposedly, could prevent drunkenness and protect people from contagious diseases. Rock crystal spheres have been used to foretell the future. Quartz does in fact have properties that make it seem magical. When quartz crystals are squeezed, they become electrically charged. And if you run an electrical current through a piece of quartz, the crystal will vibrate at a single, constant frequency which is determined by the thickness of the crystal and the strength of the current. This is why synthetic quartz crystals are used to regulate watch movements and the electronic frequencies of radios.

Quartz may be the oldest gemstone known to man. In Europe, rock crystal objects have been unearthed with the remains of prehistoric man (20,000 BC). Archaeologists have found amethyst beads, seals and good luck charms in Egypt which date back to before 3100 BC.

Due to their abundance, quartz gemstones are quite affordable. Amethyst, the most expensive variety, might retail from $2 to $90 per carat depending on quality and cut. Even amethysts that sell for $15 per carat can look good. Mineralogists classify amethyst as a variety of **crystalline** or **crystallized quartz**—quartz which occurs as regular crystals or as coarse aggregates—clusters of crystals that are often visible to the naked eye. Quartz may also be composed of crystals so tiny they can only be seen if you view a thin slice of the stone under high magnification and polarized light. This quartz is called **chalcedony** or more technically **cryptocrystalline** or **microcrystalline quartz**. Chalcedony is discussed in a separate section. Crystallized quartz (generally referred to as simply quartz) has the following properties:

RI: 1.544–1.553 (constant)	SG: 2.64–2.66	Hardness: 7	Crystal System Trigonal
Pleochroism: weak to moderate	**Toughness:** Good	**Optic Character:** DR uniaxial positive or AGG	
Cleavage: 4 good cleavages e. Rock crystal and aggregates show none.			
Reaction to Heat: Strong heat may change the color of amethyst, rose quartz and smoky quartz. Sudden temperature changes can cause fracturing or cleaving.			
Stability to Light: Some rose quartz and amethyst may fade.			
Care Tips: Ultrasonics are usually safe, but use caution. Avoid acids, alkalies, steamers and strong heat.			
Treatments: Citrine—usually heated; amethyst, ametrine & smoky quartz—sometimes heated; smoky quartz—commonly irradiated; rose quartz—sometimes irradiated; tiger's eye: commonly heated or dyed			

Quartz Varieties & Trade Names

AMETHYST (Purple or violet quartz): The most expensive color is an intense, deep, evenly-colored purple with flashes of red under incandescent light, and the least costly is pale lavender. High-clarity amethyst is readily available at low prices. Four major sources are Brazil, Uruguay, Bolivia and Zambia. A lot of synthetic amethyst, citrine and other colors of synthetic quartz are

Fig. Am.1 85-carat ametrine briolette. *Pendant from Cynthia Renée Co; photo by Colladay.*

Fig. Am.2 Rock crystal dancer with opal and diamond accents. *Brooch designed and carved by Peggy Croft; photo by Harold & Erica Van Pelt.*

Fig. Am.3 Citrine pendant created and photographed by Linda Quinn

Fig. Am.4 Flower pins carved from aventurine and rose quartz made in Japan and especially in Russia. Some amethyst is heated to lighten its color or to transform it into citrine and sometimes green quartz. Green and yellow quartz can be irradiated to produce amethyst. Amethyst may fade from heat treatment or long exposure to sunlight.

AMETRINE (Purple- and yellow-zoned quartz, i.e. amethyst + citrine): This popular gem is mined commercially in Bolivia and has only been available since the late 1980's. Its two colors allow cutters to create stones and sculptures with striking zonal patterns. Ametrine ranges in price from about $2–$40 per carat, depending on size and quality.

AVENTURINE: A translucent to opaque rock called quartzite (technically, a polycrystalline aggregate of quartz grains) with a glittery effect often caused by mica inclusions. Aventurine is typically green, but it may also be gray, yellow or brown.

CITRINE (Yellow or orange quartz): Most citrine is heat-treated amethyst or smoky quartz. Natural-color citrine is rare and is usually pale yellow. Its name is derived from the French word for lemon—*citron*. A lot of citrine is sold as topaz. It sells for around $2–$60 per carat.

QUARTZ CAT'S-EYE: Sri-Lanka, India and Brazil are sources of quartz cat's-eye. It may be white, green, yellow or brown. Cat's-eye quartz ranges from about $4–$50 per cabochon.

ROCK CRYSTAL (Colorless quartz): This is the most widely distributed variety of quartz. Nowadays, the term *crystal* by itself usually means fine-quality glass, but technically it is transparent, colorless quartz. *Crystal* comes from the Greek word for ice. Besides being cut as beads and faceted stones, rock crystal is used for lenses and all sorts of decorative objects. Once in awhile, it is quench-crackled (heated and cooled immediately) and then dyed green or red to imitate emerald and ruby.

ROSE QUARTZ (Pink quartz): This quartz, which is typically translucent, is sometimes irradiated to intensify its color and costs about $2–$25 per stone. Occasionally, it shows a star effect.

RUTILATED QUARTZ: Colorless transparent quartz that has needle-like inclusions of a mineral called rutile. Most of it comes from Brazil, and some is from Madagascar. Commercial quality cabs from Brazil retail for about $1–$3 per carat. When cut into unusual shapes, rutilated quartz can sell for up to $150 per piece. Exceptional pieces cut by expert cutters have sold for as much as $1500. Specimens with the rutile in the form of a star are the most highly valued.

SMOKY QUARTZ (Brown to black quartz): Even though smoky quartz is found worldwide, some of it on the market is irradiated rock crystal and this tends to be very dark. When it is from the Cairngorm mountains of Scotland, it is called **Cairngorm**. This quartz is often sold incorrectly under the misnomer "smoky topaz." Prices can range from around $2–$25 per stone.

TIGER'S-EYE: A translucent to opaque quartz with a silky luster and brown and gold stripes. (Technically, it's a quartz replacement of a type of asbestos called crocidolite.) Stones cut *en cabochon* with a gold band along the center resemble a cat's-eye due to the fibrous structure of the stone. South Africa is the most important source of tiger's-eye. It sells for about $3–$70 per stone. A grayish-blue quartz with a similar cat's-eye effect is called **HAWK'S-EYE**. A unique brecciated type of tiger's eye with colors that move from brown to blue to gold is found in Namibia and is sold under the name **PIETERSITE**.

Fig. Am.5 Citrine and ametrines cut by Arthur Lee Anderson. *Rings and pendants created by Gordon Aatlo; photo by Lee-Carraher.*

Fig. Am.6 Citrine and smoky quartz pendant created & photographed by Diamond Dove.

Fig. Am.7 Pietersite. *Pendant by Tom DeGasperis; photo by Shelly Smith.*

Fig. Am.8 Tiger's eye cabochon on a flattened tiger's eye oval

Fig. Am.9 Brooch made from rutilated quartz and black drusy onyx. *Created and photographed by Linda Quinn.*

Fig. Am.10 Amethyst ring. *Design by Mieke Govaerts: photo from Extrême Gioielli.*

Chalcedony SiO_2—Silica (Microcrystalline quartz)

Bloodstone—March Birthstone; Sardonyx—August birthstone; Onyx—7th wedding anniversary

Designers love gem varieties of chalcedony (cal CED nee). Its unique patterns and color combinations allow them to create attractive jewelry pieces that are unique. Chalcedony is affordable, very durable and suitable for fine carving. Besides being used in jewelry, it's also fashioned into bowls, vases, figurines, paper weights and other decorative articles.

Chalcedony is a confusing term because it has three different meanings. It can refer to a species of the quartz group—called microcrystalline or cryptocrystalline quartz (quartz composed of microscopic-size crystals). It can be a *sub*-category of microcrystalline quartz—the type whose crystal components look like sub-parallel to divergent fibers rather than grains like those of many jaspers, and chalcedony can indicate a specific variety of chalcedony that is plain white, gray or bluish gray. Properties of chalcedony are listed below:

RI: 1.53–1.54	SG: 2.58–2.64; some jasper 2.9	Hardness: 6.5–7	Toughness: Very good
Cleavage: None	Crystal System: Trigonal	Pleochroism: None	Optic Character: AGG
Reaction to Heat: The color may change depending on the cause of color.			
Stability to Light: Usually stable, but stones dyed with organic dyes can fade.			
Care Tips: Ultrasonics are usually safe. Avoid strong heat and acids.			
Treatments: Agate is commonly dyed; jasper is occasionally dyed; black onyx is always dyed, carnelian is usually heated.			

Varieties & Trade Names

AGATE: Dealers tend to apply the term agate to any patterned chalcedony that is translucent or semi-translucent, as opposed to jasper which is usually opaque to the naked eye. In a more strict usage, agate is a chalcedony with curved or angular bands (layers) of color. The bands may be multicolored or similar in color. Certain types of colorless or gray agates from Brazil and Madagascar are often stained (permanently dyed) red, black, green, blue or yellow with stable, inorganic chemicals. The main cutting and processing center for agate is Idar-Oberstein in Germany, where a lot of agate used to be mined. Now it is shipped there from Brazil and Madagascar. Other sources of agate are the U.S., Mexico, Russia and India.

Some white, gray or colorless chalcedony with inclusions is called agate. **MOSS AGATE** has moss-like green, brown, and/or red inclusions. **DENDRITIC AGATE (LANDSCAPE AGATE)** has dark inclusions that resemble trees or ferns.

Agate formed in cavities may have a crystallized crust of tiny quartz crystals (e.g. geode). This agate is called **DRUSY AGATE** or **DRUSY CHALCEDONY.**

BLOODSTONE (HELIOTROPE): An opaque dark green chalcedony with orange or red spots, which some Christians thought represented the blood of Jesus Christ. Bloodstone used to be prescribed as a cure for all types of bleeding. The injured or sick person would either wear it or place it over the affected area and the bleeding was supposed to stop. India is the main source of bloodstone. Retail prices range from about $5 to $50 per stone in sizes from 3x5mm to 15x20mm.

Fig. Ca.1 Chalcedony carved and photographed by William Cox Gem Carvings.

Fig. Ca.2 Black onyx earrings by Richard Kimball. *Photo by Steve Ramsey.*

Fig. Ca.3 Imperial jasper from Tom DeGasperis. *Photo by Shelly Smith.*

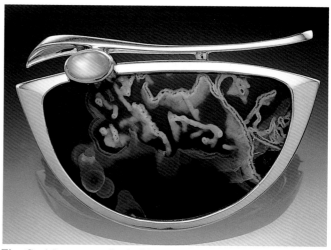

Fig. Ca.4 Lace agate backed by black onyx. *Pin by Fred & Kate Pearce; photo by Kate Pearce.*

Fig. CA.5 Moss agate from India

Fig. CA.6 Bloodstone

Fig. Ca.7 Chrysocolla: left, from Mexico; right, from Peru.

CARNELIAN (CORNELIAN in the UK**):** Translucent orange or red chalcedony. Essentially all material sold as carnelian is heat-treated or stained and heated chalcedony. Brownish red to brown chalcedony is called **SARD**. There's no distinct dividing line between sard and carnelian. Both varieties are found in Brazil and Uruguay. You can find them for sale for about $2–$30 per stone.

CHALCEDONY: White, gray or bluish gray chalcedony. Some of the main deposits are in Brazil, Madagascar, India and the U.S. It retails for about $1–$20 per stone.

BLUE CHALCEDONY: Blue material from Namibia and other localities is currently very popular and usually sells by the carat weight. It ranges in retail price from about $5–$30 per carat.

CHRYSOCOLLA QUARTZ: Blue or blue-green chalcedony that is colored blue by copper and a small amount of the mineral chrysocolla. Chrysocolla quartz can be confused with chalcedony that has been stained blue. It retails for around $10–$50 per carat.

CHRYSOCOLLA GEM SILICA: An even-colored, very translucent quality of chrysocolla quartz. It's also called **GEM CHRYSOCOLLA** or **GEM SILICA** and ranges in price from about $50 to $300 per carat retail. Much of the best quality is found near Globe, Arizona.

CHRYSOPRASE: Translucent light- to medium-green chalcedony, somewhat resembling jade. It used to be the most prized chalcedony variety. Since 1965, the best quality chrysoprase has come from Queensland, and more recently Western Australia. Other sources are Brazil, Poland and Kazakstan (formerly part of the Soviet Union). It retails for roughly $1–$20 per carat.

FIRE AGATE: A stone that displays an iridescent layer of thin iron oxide crystals under transparent chalcedony when it is cut and polished. Fire agate jewelry is especially suitable for men's jewelry because of its toughness and durability. You're most likely to find fire agate for sale in Arizona, New Mexico and Mexico, the areas where it's mined. It costs about $2–$70 per carat.

JASPER: An opaque, fine-grained chalcedony which is colored by foreign material. It's usually multicolored, spotted or striped but can be uniformly colored. The most common colors are red, brown, yellow, gray and green. Blue and black are more rare. Jasper is found worldwide. Jasper with patterns reminiscent of desert landscapes is called picture jasper and is particularly popular in Western American jewelry. It retails for about $5–$80 per piece and sometimes up to $250.

ONYX: Chalcedony composed of relatively straight, parallel layers of different colors. When the dark layers (bands) are brown or brownish red, it's often called **SARDONYX**. Layered onyx is ideal for cameos. It's produced when dense layers do not absorb the dye and remain white while other more porous layers take on the dyes and end up blue, green, black, etc. **BLACK ONYX** is not really onyx. It's just chalcedony that has been dyed completely black. It's priced at about $1–$30 per piece retail. Black onyx with sandblasted designs on it retails for up to $100 per piece.

PETRIFIED WOOD: (Fossilized Wood, Agatized Wood): Wood that has been replaced by chalcedony. Petrification can occur when trees are covered with fine sedimentary rock rich in volcanic ash shortly after their death. The wood does not turn into stone. It is just gradually replaced by rock which preserves the shape and structural elements of the wood. The most famous occurrence of petrified wood is at the Petrified Forest National Park in Arizona. Petrified wood can be agate, jasper or opal. Shells and bones can also undergo petrification. Some jasper in Colorado, Utah and Wyoming is petrified dinosaur bone. It's usually just sold as "dinosaur bone" or "dinny bone."

Fig. Ca.8 Chrysoprase ring by Richard Kimball. *Photo by Steve Ramsey*

Fig. Ca.9 Left, jasper; right, agate. *Pins from Timeless Gem Designs.*

Fig. Ca.10 Gem chrysocolla from Bisbee, Arizona. Well-matched quality stones like these are hard to find. *Earrings by Michael Francis & Co; photo from Platinum Guild Intl. USA.*

Fig. Ca.11 Jasper earrings. *Design by Lori Braun; jewelry and photo copyright 1995 by Murphy Design.*

Fig. Ca.12 Carnelian

Fig. Ca.13 Picture jasper from Idaho

Fig. Ca.14 Petrified dinosaur bone & fire opal. *Pin from Fred & Kate Pearce; photo by Ralph Gabriner.*

Figs. CA 15–17 Top—lace agate; middle—poppy jasper; bottom—agate from Pearce Design. *Photos by Kate Pearce.*

Fig. Ca.18 Jasper from Tom DeGasperis. *Photo by Shelly Smith.*

Chrysoberyl (Alexandrite, Cat's Eye...) $BeAl_2O_4$—Beryllium aluminum oxide

Alexandrite—Alternate birthstone for June; Cat's-eye—18th wedding anniversary stone.

Alexandrite and cat's-eye look very different, yet they are the same mineral—chrysoberyl. A less expensive type of chrysoberyl is transparent, shows no optical effects and ranges in color from green, to yellow to brown. Thanks to their good hardness and durability, chrysoberyls are well-suited for jewelry use. Today, Brazil and Sri Lanka are the most important sources of chrysoberyls. Deposits are also found in Russia, Tanzania, Zimbabwe, Madagascar and Myanmar (Burma). Listed below are the physical and optical characteristics of chrysoberyl:

RI: 1.74–1.76	SG: 3.70–3.76	Hardness 8,5	Toughness: Good to excellent
Cleavage: Indistinct or none		DR, biaxial positive	Crystal System: Orthorhombic
Pleochroism: Strong trichroism in alexandrite, none in cat's-eye, weak to moderate in transparent yellow, green and brown varieties			
Care Tips: Ultrasonics and steamers are safe if stone has a good clarity. Stable to heat and light; no reaction to chemicals; overall, a durable natural gemstone with excellent wearability.			
Treatments: Normally none. Occasionally fractures may be masked with fillers.			

ALEXANDRITE: This gem was first discovered in the Ural mountains of Russia in 1830 on the 12th birthday of Czar Alexander II, hence the name. In its finest qualities, alexandrite looks green in sunlight and purplish-red under incandescent light (light bulbs). Coincidentally, red and green were the colors of the Russian Imperial Guard. Don't expect to find natural alexandrite in your local jewelry store—it's very rare. When you do see it for sale, the colors are likely to be a grayish green and brownish purple or lavender. Synthetic alexandrite and synthetic alexandrite-like sapphire or spinel are readily available. Prices for natural alexandrites above a carat that show a noticeable change of color start at about $1500 per carat retail and can go over $20,000 per carat depending on size and quality. The distinctness of the color change and the color intensity are the most important price factors, but size and clarity also affect the cost.

CAT'S-EYE: Treasured for centuries in the Orient, cat's-eye became popular in Europe in the late 19th century when the Duke of Connaught gave a cat's-eye engagement ring to Princess Louise Margaret of Prussia. Today, cat's-eye is used mostly in men's jewelry. Other minerals such as quartz, tourmaline and beryl may also display a cat's-eye (stripe of reflected light across a cabochon), but chrysoberyl cat's-eye is the most prized and has the sharpest eye. The unmodified term **cat's-eye** means chrysoberyl cat's-eye. Other cat's-eye stones must indicate the mineral, as for example, cat's-eye quartz or quartz cat's-eye. A brownish yellow similar to the color of honey is the most valued color, but greenish-yellow stones can also be very expensive. In the finest qualities, cat's-eye can wholesale for over $3000 per carat. Stones with fuzzy, non-sharp eyes, dull colors and eye-visible inclusions can sell for less than $100 per carat. Cat's-eye can also display a color change. Alexandrite cat's-eyes, however, are quite rare.

YELLOW, GREEN or BROWN (transparent) **CHRYSOBERYL:** Attractive and durable, high-quality yellow or green chrysoberyl is affordably priced between $100 and $500 per carat, depending on size. Unfortunately, you won't find it in many jewelry stores.

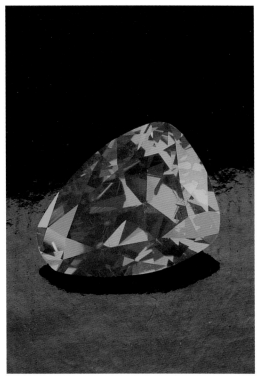

Fig. Cr.1 A 2.23 carat Russian alexandrite of unusually fine quality. Viewed under incandescent light, it appears reddish. *Stone courtesy Andrew Sarosi; photo by Robert Weldon.*

Fig. Cr.2 The same stone viewed under fluorescent light looks green. It's rare for alexandrite to show such a distinct color change. (Printed colors only approximate actual colors.) *Stone courtesy Andrew Sarosi; photo by Robert Weldon.*

Fig. Cr.3 Cat's-eye

Fig. Cr.4 Yellow and brownish-orange chrysoberyl

Emerald & Other Beryl Stones $Be_3Al_2(SiO_3)_6$—Beryllium aluminum silicate

Emerald—May birthstone; aquamarine—March birthstone; emerald—20th & 35th anniversary

In its pure form, beryl is colorless. But thanks to the presence of impurities, this mineral can be blue, green, pink, red, yellow or orange. If, for example, traces of chromium and/or vanadium are present, the result may be an emerald. A trace of iron can turn the beryl into an aquamarine, whereas a bit of manganese adds a pink or orange color to the stone.

Of all the beryls, emerald is the most highly valued and has the longest history. Some evidence indicates that emerald deposits in Egypt may have been exploited as early as 3500 BC. However, most of the Egyptian emeralds were pale, drab and heavily flawed. It wasn't until the 1500's, when the Spanish invaded the Americas, that Europeans realized how beautiful an emerald could be and vast quantities of Colombian emeralds were brought to Europe by the conquistadors.

Aquamarine and yellow beryl have also had a long history, but it's hard to determine when they were first used. The orange, pink and red beryls have only been recognized as gems since the early 1900's. Listed below are the physical and optical properties of the beryl family.

RI: 1.57–1.60	SG: 2.67–2.80	Hardness: 7.5–8	Crystal System: Hexagonal
Toughness: Poor to good depending on clarity			Optic character: DR, uniaxial negative
Pleochroism: Emerald, moderate to strong yellowish-green and bluish-green; weak to moderate dichroism in the other beryls			Cleavage: Rare and indistinct in one direction
Reaction to Heat: In emerald, it may cause fracturing or complete breakage; Maxixe and Maxixe-type beryl fade quickly at 100^0 C or higher.			
Stability to Light: Stable, except for Maxixe and Maxixe-type beryl. There can also be fading in orange beryl or in emeralds treated with green oil. In addition, orange beryl may change to pink.			
Reaction to Chemicals: Resists all acids except hydrofluoric; solvents such as acetone and alcohol may drive out fracture fillings in emerald.			
Care tips: Clean emeralds with a damp cloth or spray with window cleaner & wipe dry. Don't soak emeralds in cleaning solutions because they can dissolve fillers. Ultrasonics are usually safe for beryls of good clarity.			
Treatments: Assume that emeralds & red beryl have been fracture filled unless otherwise stated. Pink beryl and aquamarine are usually heated; yellow beryl is usually irradiated; emeralds are occasionally dyed.			

Varieties & Trade Names

EMERALD: The definition of an emerald varies depending on the user. At gem shows and in stores, any beryl that looks more or less green is typically labeled as an emerald. Some emerald dealers feel that light green stones should be called "green beryl" and that the term "emerald" should be reserved for darker stones. European mineralogists tend to believe true emeralds must be colored by chromium, whereas American gemologists feel stones colored by vanadium can also be classified as emeralds. The definition of "emerald" is irrelevant when it comes to pricing. If a one-carat beryl has a saturated green color and is transparent and eye-clean, it can be worth over $5000 retail. Top quality, 6-carat emeralds can *wholesale* for over $10,000 **per carat**. If a beryl is light green and has poor transparency, it's not worth much, no matter how it's labeled.

Fig. Em.2 A 4.33-carat Zambian emerald. *Ring and photo from Color Masters Gem Corp.*

Fig. Em.1 Aquamarine sculpted by Sherris Cottier Shank. *Photo by John McMartin.*

Fig. Em.3 Yellow beryl. *Ring and photo from Robert Trisko Jewelry Sculptures.*

Fig. Em.4 Morganite jewelry. *Gems from Cynthia Renée Co.; jewelry by Nanz Aalund; photo by Jeff Engelstad.*

Low-grade emerald or beryl can sell for as little as $10 per carat. It's normal for an emerald to be flawed with inclusions and cracks, especially if it has a deep green color. Nevertheless, clarity and transparency play a major role in emerald pricing. Emeralds are routinely treated with oil, wax or epoxy-like substances to hide cracks and improve transparency. This is considered an acceptable trade practice as long as it is disclosed. Some fillers are more stable than others, but it's usually not possible for salespeople to know exactly what an emerald has been filled with. Lab documents, however, can provide you with information on the extent and type of filling. Reputable jewelers will stand behind their emeralds, and many will retreat the stones if necessary. For a fuller discussion of emerald treatments, quality evaluation and identification, consult the *Ruby, Sapphire & Emerald Buying Guide* by Renée Newman.

Colombia is the most important source of top-grade emerald. High-quality emerald is also found in Zambia, Zimbabwe, Brazil and Pakistan, but not in the same quantities as in Colombia. Other deposits include Russia, Afghanistan, Australia, India and North Carolina.

GREEN BERYL: There is no agreed-upon criterion in the trade for distinguishing between green beryl and emerald. Likewise, there is no clear dividing line between green beryl and aquamarine.

AQUAMARINE: The name "aquamarine" means "sea water" in Latin, alluding to its color. Most natural-color aquamarine is light bluish-green. Prior to the 1900's, this was the preferred color for aquamarine. Today it's routinely heat-treated to remove the green component, thereby producing a permanently-colored blue stone. The more intense the blue color, the more valuable the stone. Aquamarines usually have a high transparency and clarity, even under magnification. They're also very durable and their color is evenly distributed. Fine quality stones over a carat retail for about $200–$1000 per carat. Brazil is the most important producer of aquamarine. Madagascar, Mozambique, Ukraine, Nigeria, Pakistan and Zambia are other major sources.

MAXIXE BERYL: This beryl has a medium to dark color resembling sapphire. It was named after the mine in Brazil where it was discovered around 1917. Since then, a similar stone has appeared on the market called Maxixe-type beryl. It is produced by irradiating pale pink or colorless beryl. Maxixe and Maxixe-type beryls are rare and they fade when exposed to light.

HELIODOR (YELLOW BERYL): Found in Madagascar, Brazil, Russia, Namibia and the U.S., this beryl is not uncommon. It's also been called golden beryl. It retails for about $50–$350 ct.

MORGANITE (PINK, ORANGE or PURPLE BERYL): Morganite was named after the famous financier J. P. Morgan. The first morganite to be described was a pale pink variety found in California. Some of the finest, most intensely-colored morganite is found in Madagascar. Brazil is another important source, but the colors are usually lighter even though the crystals are much larger. To intensify the color, morganite is commonly heat-treated. It can retail for $40–$500 ct.

RED BERYL (BIXBITE): This valuable beryl was discovered in Utah in 1906. Red beryl is sometimes erroneously called red emerald. Due to its rarity, it remains a collector gem.

GOSHENITE (COLORLESS BERYL): Goshenite is named after Goshen, Massachusetts, where it was first found. It has been used to imitate diamond or emerald by placing silver or green colored metal foil behind it in a closed back setting. Goshenite is not common.

CAT'S-EYE BERYL: Chatoyancy is most likely to occur in aquamarine and morganite. However, cat's-eye emerald and cat's-eye yellow beryl also exist. These are collector stones.

Fig. Em.6 Colombian emeralds. *Photo and jewelry from Harry Winston, Inc.*

Fig. Em.5 A ring-shaped aquamarine (Torus Ring™) carved & photographed by Glenn Lehrer

Fig. Em.7 Heliodor (yellow beryl)

Fig. Em.8 Maxixe-type beryl. *Photo by Robert Weldon.*

Garnet (a group of gem species)

January birthstone and 2nd wedding anniversary stone

Friendship—this is what the garnet represents. According to legend, adorning yourself with garnets will improve your personal relationships and protect you from harm. These benefits are doubled if your birthday is in January. Traditionally, people have considered garnets to be red, but they can also be various shades of green, yellow, orange, brown, pink or purple.

The word "garnet" comes from the Latin *granatum* meaning "seedlike." Garnet crystals in rock reminded early scientists of the shape and color of pomegranate seeds.

Historical accounts and findings suggest that garnet beads and inlaid jewelry were worn in Egypt as early as 3100 BC. Tracing the history of gemstones is difficult because they were often misidentified. It's certain, though, that during the 18th and 19th centuries, garnets were popular in Europe. The bourgeoisie would buy these stones while vacationing in the hot springs of Bohemia, Czechoslovakia, and take them home as souvenirs and good luck charms. Until the late 1800's, Bohemia was the world's major source of pyrope garnet (a garnet species).

Below is a chart which lists various members of the garnet group. Much of the data is from *Gems* by Robert Webster. Keep in mind that garnets are almost always a mixture of different garnet species and have varying properties. The species name refers to the main component of a garnet. Use this table as a general guide only; the RI, SG and hardness values may be higher or lower than indicated, and there can be a wide variation of color within a given species. One garnet species, uvarovite, was not included because it's usually too small to be cut into gemstones. However, a drusy form has been on the market since the late 1990's (see fig. 2.45, page 31).

Species	Varieties	Basic Color	RI	SG	Hardness
Andradite	Demantoid Topazolite Melanite	Green Yellow / orange Black	1.88–1.89	3.81–3.87	6 1/2–7
Spessartine	Kashmirine Little Three Mine Mandarin garnet	Orange Orange Orange	1.78 – 1.81	4.12–4.20	7 1/4
Almandine (if pure) Almandine		Purple Purple	1.83 1.78–1.83	4.25 3.95–4.25	7 1/2 7 1/4
Pyrope-almandine	Rhodolite	Purple-red / pink	1.75–1.78	3.80–3.95	7 1/4
Pyrope Pyrope (if pure)		Red Red	1.73–1.75 1.71	3.65–3.80 3.51	7 1/4 7 1/4
Grossular-andradite	Mali garnet	Green or yellow	1.75–1.78	3.64–3.68	
Pyrope-spessartine	Color change & Malaia garnet	Variable Orange / pink-orange	1.74–1.78	3.78–3.85	7 1/4
Grossular	Hessonite Tsavorite Translucent green Translucent white Translucent pink	Orange or yellow Green Green White Pink	1.74–1.76 1.74–1.76 1.72–1.73 1.72–1.73 1.70–1.73	3.59–3.65 3.57–3.64 3.42–3.50 3.45–3.50 3.35–3.41	7 1/4 7 1/4 7 7 7

Fig. G.1 Demantoid garnet ring from Cynthia Renée Co. *Photo by Robert Weldon.*

Fig. G.2 A 4.48 ct-spessartite garnet flanked by two tsavorites. *Ring by Gary Dulac; photo copyright 1994 by Azad.*

Fig. G.3 Green grossularite pendant by Mark Schneider. *Photo by Daniel Van Rossen.*

Fig. G.4 Melanite (black andradite) from Gary Dulac. *Photo by Azad.*

Fig. G.5 Rhodolite garnet ring from Cynthia Renée Co. *Photo by Robert Weldon.*

Fig. G.6 A Sri Lankan rhodolite garnet (35.30 cts) from Cynthia Renée Co. *Photo by Robert Weldon*

Jewelers normally identify lower priced garnets as simply garnets. It's not worth the time and money to test the stones and determine their species category. Properties shared by the various garnets are listed below.

Crystal System: Cubic (isometric)	**Cleavage**: None, but may have indistinct parting
Toughness: Fair to good	**Optic Character**: Singly refractive, anomalous double refraction
Treatments: Normally none	**Reaction to Heat**: Sudden temperature changes can cause fractures
Care Tips: Ultrasonics are usually safe with stones of good clarity; avoid thermal shock,	

Species, Varieties & Trade Names

ANDRADITE $(Ca_3Fe_2(SiO_4)_3)$: The best known andradite variety is **DEMANTOID**, which was discovered in 1868 in the Ural Mountain area of Russia. It resembles an emerald with added brilliance and fire. Its fire (dispersion) is greater than that of any other natural gemstone, including diamond. The name "demantoid" comes from the Old German word *demant* meaning diamond-like. A lot of Victorian gemstone jewelry made between 1885 and 1915 featured demantoid.

Good demantoid is not easy to find today. For more than 80 years, most of the ·mining in Russia ceased, but the Russians are now producing it again. Recent finds in Namibia have made it more available. Some demantoid is also mined in Mexico, Italy, Czechoslovakia and Arizona, but the color tends to be yellowish. Asbestos-fiber inclusions resembling horsetails are considered a positive feature in demantoid. Their presence strongly suggests the stones are from the Russian Ural region, which has also been the source of some high-quality alexandrite. The retail price of demantoid weighing one carat or more can range from about $400 to over $6000 per carat.

The opaque black variety of andradite, **MELANITE**, has been used in mourning jewelry. The crystals of **TOPAZOLITE**, a yellow variety, are rare and typically small.

SPESSARTINE or **SPESSARTITE** $(Mn_3Al_2(SiO_4)_3)$: This species can be yellowish orange to reddish orange or brownish orange. The most valued color is orange with red overtones. Sources include Sri Lanka, Brazil, Afghanistan, Myanmar, Madagascar, East Africa and California. One place that's particularly noted for high-quality spessartine is the Little Three Mine in California. Spessartine mined in Namibia is usually called **mandarin garnet**. Spessartine from Kashmir is named **Kashmirine**. Retail prices of top-grade material can be as high as $1400 per carat. Most spessartines on the market, though, tend to sell for about $5 to $200 per carat.

ALMANDINE or **ALMANDITE** $(Fe_3Al_2(SiO_4)_3)$: Much of the material which is sold as almandine is low-priced pyrope (garnet composed mostly of pyrope with some almandine and grossular). This leads people to believe that almandine is more plentiful than it actually is. Opinions differ as to how almandine should be defined. At the very least, the chief component should be almandine. But mineralogists disagree on how much almandine should be present and what its properties should be. According to noted gemologist Robert Webster (*Gems*, p. 174), the bottom limits for the refractive index and specific gravity of almandine are 1.78 and 3.95. However, these figures are arbitrary. Almandines of high purity are rare and typically have a

Fig. G.5 Top left to right: Mali garnet, hessonite. Bottom left to right: spessartine garnet, grossular garnet.

Fig. G.6 Pyrope garnet ring by Dan Miller. *Photo by Luciano Baldi.*

Fig. G.7 Tsavorite garnet. *Ring by Proprioro; photo by TKO Studios.*

purplish color. They range from about $3 to $100 per carat. Sources include Sri Lanka, India, Brazil, Australia, Tanzania, Madagascar and the U.S. Star almandine is found in Idaho. These star garnets usually have four rays but six rays may be seen in certain directions of some stones.

RHODOLITE (Pyrope-almandine): Rhodolite was discovered in 1882 in North Carolina. Those deposits have been depleted, but since then it has been found in Africa, Brazil, India and Sri Lanka. Tanzania is the major commercial source. The name of this purplish-red garnet comes from the Greek *rhodo* (rose) and *lithos* (stone). Rhodolites can range in price from $5 to $300 per carat retail. Top-quality stones are clean, very transparent and saturated in color but not dark.

PYROPE (PIE rope) ($Mg_3Al_2(SiO_4)_3$): This garnet's name is derived from the Greek *pyropos* meaning "fire-like," alluding to its deep red color. Pyrope is found throughout the world, with some of the best quality coming from the diamond mines of South Africa. As a result, it has sometimes been referred to as "cape ruby." "Arizona ruby" is a misnomer for pyrope from Arizona. Pyrope is a very affordable stone with retail prices ranging from about $3 to $100 per carat. The redder the stone, the more valuable it is. Eye-clean material is readily available.

MALI GARNET or **GRANDITE** (Grossular-andradite): Marketed only since 1995, Mali garnets are found in western Africa in the Republic of Mali. They can be various shades of green, yellow or brown. These "new" garnets often resemble faceted chrysoberyl, and their prices are similar.

MALAIA (MALAYA): Consisting mostly of pyrope-spessartine, this distinctive orange variety may be reddish, pinkish or yellowish. It was found in East Africa in the search for rhodolite, a purplish-red garnet coveted in Japan. Pinkish orange and orange with overtones of red are the most valued malaia colors. Top qualities can retail for up to $600 whereas low-grade malaia can sell for as little as $10 per carat. In Europe, gemologists often refer to it as **umbalite**. "Malaia" is the Swahili word for "outcast" or "prostitute."

   COLOR-CHANGE GARNET is found in many different colors and displays a variation of color behavior. For example, it may be blue or green in daylight and reddish in incandescent light. Color-change garnet consists mainly of pyrope-spessartine with some grossular.

GROSSULAR or **GROSSULARITE** ($Ca_3Al_2(SiO_4)_3$): The most valued variety of this species is **TSAVORITE** (also **tsavolite**), a transparent green garnet. It was discovered in Tanzania in 1968. Later it was also found in Kenya, and promoters from Tiffany & Co. named it after the country's Tsavo National Park. Tsavorite is found in almost all shades of green but tends to be yellowish-green. When its color resembles that of fine emerald, it can retail for over $3000 per carat in sizes over 3 carats. Retail prices of smaller commercial quality stones can drop down to $100 per carat. Grossular that is light green and transparent is typically called green grossular.

   HESSONITE is a much less expensive variety of grossular that is sometimes called **cinnamon stone**. The colors are often brownish and can be red, orange, yellow or colorless. When viewed under magnification, hessonite typically has a granular "heat wave" appearance. There are hessonite deposits in Sri Lanka, the U.S., Canada, Madagascar, Siberia and Brazil.

   Translucent and opaque grossular is used for beads, cabochons and carvings. The green material (technically named **hydrogrossular**) is sometimes called **Transvaal jade**, after its main source in South Africa. It has also been found in the USSR, Hungary and Italy. Small black inclusions (black specks) are a characteristic of this green grossular. Translucent pink grossular, mixed in white marble, is found mainly in Mexico and is sometimes called **rosolite**, after its color.

Iolite (Cordierite species) $Mg_2Al_4Si_5O_{18}$—a complex silicate of magnesium and aluminum

21st wedding anniversary stone

Before the 1980's, iolite was mainly considered a collector's stone because so little of it was being sold. Today, it is more readily available, and it is often used as a sapphire or tanzanite substitute due to its blue-violet color and lower price. You can find high-quality iolite for less than $200 per carat retail. Overly dark and flawed stones sell for much less.

Mineralogists call the stone **cordierite**, a name given to the mineral in honor of French geologist Pierre Cordier. The name iolite was derived from the Greek word for violet, *ios*. Some people have referred to iolite as **water sapphire** because it resembles sapphire face-up and it looks clear or watery from the side. This effect is due to the strong trichroism of iolite. In one direction the crystal typically appears dark blue or violet; in another it is colorless, gray or yellowish; and in a third direction it is light blue or violet.

Iolite has also been referred to as the "Viking's compass." On cloudy days, the Vikings were able to locate the position of the sun by looking through thin colorless slices of iolite. The stone acted as a light polarizer and canceled out haze and mist.

The Vikings probably got their iolite from Greenland or Norway, but today most of it comes from India, Sri Lanka, Tanzania and Brazil. Additional sources include Myanmar, Madagascar, Zimbabwe and Namibia. The physical and optical properties of iolite are listed below.

RI: 1.53–1.58	SG: 2.56–2.66	Hardness: 7–7.5	Crystal System: Orthorhombic
Toughness: fair	**Trichroism:** strong	**Optic Character:** DR, biaxial negative	
Treatments: normally not treated		**Cleavage:** Distinct in one direction	
Reaction to heat: fusible		**Reaction to Chemicals:** Attacked by acids	
Care tips: Ultrasonics are risky; avoid acids and sudden temperature changes.			

Fig. I.1 Iolite ring from Proprioro. *TKO studios.*

Fig. I.2 Emerald-cut iolite

Jade (Jadeite & Nephrite)
12th wedding anniversary stone

...jade is a possession to be cherished by anyone who can find it or buy it or steal it. Chinese women ask for jade ornaments for their hair, and old men keep in their closed palms a piece of cool jade, so smooth that it seems soft to the touch. Rich men buy jades instead of putting their money in banks, for jade grows more beautiful with age.
Pearl S. Buck, *My Several Worlds*

There is no other stone that is as resistant to breakage and chipping as jade. This inherent toughness made it a superior weapon and tool for early man. To him it meant survival, and its colors were reminiscent of nature. As a result, jade became known as a gift from heaven. It was even more esteemed than diamonds or gold by some civilizations in Asia, Central America and the South Pacific.

According to the great Chinese philosopher Confucius, jade was highly valued for a variety of reasons—its polish and brilliancy represent the whole of purity; its compactness and hardness represent the sureness of the intelligence; the pure and prolonged sound which it gives forth when one strikes it represents music; its color represents loyalty (from *Jade: Stone of Heaven* by Richard Gump, pg 23). Today jade is worn by millions of Orientals for good luck and health, and it is given to celebrate all important occasions in life such as births, marriages, anniversaries and business agreements.

The Spanish conquistadors are credited for giving us the term "jade." When they learned that natives in Mexico were wearing jade to relieve kidney ailments, they called it *piedra de ijada* meaning "stone of the loins." Gradually, the Spanish term evolved to "jade." The early Romans had also considered jade to be a good cure for kidney ailments such as nephritis (kidney inflammation) and called jade *lapis nephriticus*—"stone of nephrite." Later the Latin term was reduced to "nephrite" and was used as an alternate word for jade. In 1863, the French chemist Augustine Damour realized that jade was two different minerals, so he coined the word **jadeite** for Burmese jade to distinguish it from Chinese jade—**nephrite**. The Chinese had been aware of the difference between the two jades since the mid 1700's.

Jadeite and nephrite are both rocks (aggregates)—masses of tightly interlocking crystals, rather than single crystals like most gems. However, they have different chemical compositions and properties. Jadeite is a little harder and denser, and as a result can take a higher polish than nephrite. Neither stone is very hard, compared to diamond. ruby and sapphire. However, both jades are unusually tough—resistant to breakage and chipping. Valuable jade carvings, for example, have survived falls in earthquakes when other hard objects nearby have not. Nephrite, however, is slightly stronger, due to its intergrown, fiberlike crystal components. Jadeite is made up of crystals which tend to be more granular and more coarse. These are sometimes visible without magnification.

Jadeite is more valuable and rare than nephrite. Myanmar (Burma) has been the main source of jadeite since the late 18th century, when China began to import jade from there. Prior to that time, Guatemalan jadeite had been used extensively in Central America by Indians such as the Aztecs and the Mayas. Some jadeite is also mined in Russia, Japan and California; but the finest quality comes from Myanmar. When it is very translucent and has a strong emerald-green color, it is often called **Imperial jade**. Jadeite is found in a variety of colors—lavender, white, gray, yellow, orange, brownish-red, black and many shades of green. Today, jadeite is usually the jade chosen for fine jewelry. Its intrinsic value is generally the basis for its price. Nephrite, on the other hand, is mainly valued for its antiquity and carving excellence.

Nephrite is plentiful and most of it is grayish green—typically forest green or olive green. It can also be white, gray, black, brown, yellow or beige. The oldest known source of nephrite is

Fig. J.1 Green jade. *Jewelry & photo from Mason-Kay.*

Fig. J.2 "Red Jade." *Photo from Mason-Kay.*

Center left: **Fig J.3** Black jade and fire opal pendant/slide hand-fabricated by Gary Dulac. *Photo by John Parrish.*

Bottom left: **Fig. J.4** Guatemalan jadeite pendant slide by Fred & Kate Pearce. *Photo by Kate Pearce.*

Bottom right: **Fig J.5** Siberian jade carved by Michael Francis. *Photo by Christa Lauren Kuether.*

Xinjiang Province in China (formerly Eastern Turkestan). For centuries, this is where China got its jade. The nephrite found in Xinjiang tends to be light in color. Although it is usually thought of as an oriental stone, nephrite was also mined and carved in ceremonial fashion by other cultures throughout history—notably the Maoris of New Zealand. Nephrite is also found in Taiwan, British Columbia, Australia, Poland, Germany, India, Zimbabwe, Mexico, Alaska, California and Wyoming. The chemical composition and properties of nephrite and jadeite can be compared by referring to the two charts below:

Jadeite $NaAl(Si_2O_6)$—Sodium aluminum silicate			
RI: 1.66–1.68	**SG:** 3.30–3.36	**Hardness:** 6.5–7	**Toughness:** Exceptional
Crystal System: Monoclinic		**Optic Character:** AGG (DR) biaxial positive	
Care Tips: Ultrasonics are not advised for treated jade. Avoid chemicals and high heat.			
Treatments: Commonly bleached, treated with polymers and dyed. Sometimes heated; usually waxed.			

Nephrite $Ca_2(Mg,Fe)_5(Si_4O_{11})_2(OH)_2$—Calcium magnesium iron silicate			
RI: 1.60–1.63	**SG:** 2.90–3.05	**Hardness** 6–6.5	**Toughness:** Exceptional, even better than jadeite
Crystal System: Monoclinic		**Optic Character:** AGG (DR) biaxial positive	
Care Tips: Ultrasonics & steamers are safe for untreated stones. Avoid acids & heat from jeweler's torch			
Treatments: Often not treated, except for waxing. Sometimes dyed or heated.			

Evaluation of Jade

Color: An intense green with a medium to medium-dark tone is the most valued. As the color becomes lighter, darker, more grayish or brownish or yellowish, the value decreases. Lavender is the next most valued hue, followed by red, yellow, white and black. Prior to the importation of Burmese jadeite into China, white nephrite was the jade most coveted by Chinese royalty.

Color Uniformity: In top quality jade, the color is uniform throughout the stone. The more uneven or blotchy the color is, the lower the value. Multi-colored jade, however, can be very expensive if the colors are intense and distinct. The most desired color combinations are green and lavender, orange and green, or white with strong green (**moss-in-snow** jade).

Transparency: The best jade is either semi-transparent or highly translucent. In his book *Jade for You*, jade dealer John Ng says jade can even be near transparent. It's called **water jade, "glass" jade** or **crystal jade**, whereas semi-transparent jade may be labeled **honey jade**. As the transparency of jade decreases, so does its value, with opaque jade being worth the least. Many jade dealers use the term **translucency** instead of "transparency." For the sake of consistency, this book uses the term "transparency" when categorizing the degree to which light passes through gems.

Fig. J.6 Top-quality green and lavender jadeite. Today, fine material like this is cut into cabochons. *Jewelry from Mason-Kay; photo by Richard Rubins.*

Fig. J.7 Spinach jadeite (dark-green jade) skillfully cut into a swan—it was difficult to create such symmetrical veins and feathers. Formerly, jade pieces were often carved for aesthetic reasons; today, they're carved to remove imperfections. Consequently, smooth jade is now more valuable than carved jade. *Brooch and photo from Mason-Kay.*

Fig. J.8 This jadeite cabochon is very translucent and has a superb polish, but its color is a little too light for it to qualify as top-quality jade. Nevertheless, the stone wholesaled for $40,000 in 1997. *Jade & photo from Mason-Kay.*

Fig. J.9 Nephrite jewelry from British Columbia. The dark green jade is a typical nephrite color. The lighter green is not so common and is more in demand in the Orient as a nephrite color.

Clarity: Fine jade is free of flaws such as cracks, included foreign material, cloudy areas, streaks and spots which reduce beauty or durability. The number, size, color, position and nature of flaws determines the clarity of a stone. Fractures that break the surface or that are visible internally are particularly detrimental to the value of jade.

Texture: Jade can have a texture that ranges from fine to coarse. That's because it is composed of intergrown crystals. The finer and more tightly interwoven the crystal components are, the better the jade.

Shape: The best quality jade is cut into cabochons. Ovals and rounds normally sell for more than rectangular, marquise and pear shapes. Smooth uncarved pieces are more valuable than carved ones. Carving allows the removal of flaws from inferior material.

Size: Since large, fine quality jadeite is rare, size does play a role in increasing its value. The thickness of good jadeite is also important. If a jadeite cabochon is thinner than 2mm or smaller than 8 x 6 mm, there can be a considerable deduction in its per-carat value.

Polish & Finish: The more brilliant the polish and the smoother the surface, the better the stone is. Every scratch, sharp angle and rough surface should be removed during the polishing process. When stones lose their luster and become scratched, they can be repolished. Texture and polish are related because fine-textured stones can take a higher polish than those with a coarse texture. Hardness is also important. Since nephrite is a little softer, it normally does not take as high of a polish as jadeite.

Jade Treatments

Waxing: This treatment is considered acceptable in the trade. It's commonly done after the final polish to improve luster and hide pits and cracks. The stone is soaked in a colorless molten wax and then buffed to achieve a good shine. Heat and strong solvents will undo this treatment. Material which has received only a superficial waxing is often called **A jade** in the trade.

Dyeing: This is often done to add green or lavender color to white or light-colored jade. The stone is heated to open up the "pores" and then dye is forced into it often with high pressure. Blueberry juice is a common dye for lavender jade. It looks good at first but it can fade in sunlight. Gemologists use a microscope and a spectroscope to detect dyes, but even with these instruments, dyes may be hard to detect. Dyed jade is called **C Jade**.

Heating: Dark green nephrite may be treated by this method to lighten the color of dark-green material. Red jade can be heated to increase redness, but the usual result is a dull brown, and transparency is reduced in the process.

Bleaching and polymer impregnation: This relatively new treatment removes brown from jade, making white colors whiter and green colors brighter. The jade is first soaked and bleached in chemicals. Microscopic tunnels are created as silica is removed during the process. Then the bleached jade is impregnated with a synthetic material to fill these tunnels. The resulting material is called **B jade**. Sometimes dye is used before impregnation and other times it is added to the filler. An article in the Fall 1992 issue of *Gems & Gemology* (pp. 176-187) discusses various tests for this treatment. The only definitive test is infrared spectroscopy, which requires sophisticated equipment that few gem labs have. Don't plan on handing bleached jade down to future genera-

Fig. J.10 An assortment of jadeite bangles and rings. Hinged bangles sell better in western countries, but all other factors being equal, they are less valued than one-piece bangles. The green and white jade in the one-piece bangle is referred to as "moss-in-snow." *Photo and jewelry from Mason-Kay.*

Fig. J.11 Black nephrite and dark gray jadeite. *Courtesy Mason-Kay.*

Fig. J.12 Jadeite carving. If it were completely green, it would be worth more. If it were all lavender, it would be worth less. *Jade and photo from Mason-Kay.*

tions; it will discolor with time and the tiny tunnels create durability problems. Prongs from mountings can dig into the "B jade," and dish-washing solutions and other substances can damage it over time. Sellers are supposed to disclose treatments, especially when they are not stable, but not all do.

When buying jade, deal with reputable jewelers. Ask how and if it has been treated. Have the treatment information written on the receipt. And have expensive pieces checked by major gem labs which have the experience and equipment required to test jade.

Colors of Jadeite and Nephrite

Green Jadeite: In good qualities, this is the most expensive jade. A very fine emerald-green cab (cabochon) that is translucent, evenly colored and 13 x 18mm can wholesale for over $20,000 if the color is natural. The same quality in a 6 x 8mm size might wholesale for over $2000. As the stones become more yellowish, grayish or less intensely colored, the price goes down. A very light grayish-green cab that is 6 x 8mm can sell for as little as $25.

Jadeite value is very much a function of how it is used. The way in which beads and cabs are valued illustrates this. A $10 green jadeite cab would normally be considered low quality. A $1000 strand of fifty 8mm green jadeite beads could be considered a nice example of jade jewelry. This strand would yield 100 cabs if the beads were cut in two, making the price of each cab $10. So material that produces decent beads makes substandard cabs.

Green Nephrite: Most nephrite is very affordable. The nephrite pendant and the pair of earrings shown in figure J.9 retail for less than $20 each. The antique value of old nephrite pieces often outweighs their intrinsic worth. Green nephrite is typically grayish, blackish or brownish. The more it approaches a pure green, the more desirable it is.

Lavender Jadeite: This jadeite can range in color from a light grayish-pink to a deep purple. A top-quality intense lavender cabochon that is 13 x 10mm may wholesale for over $2500.

"Red" Jade: Most so-called red jade is orange, brown or a rust-like brownish-red. This color is found on the outside of the rough and is presumably caused by the oxidation of the iron content from the surrounding water or earth. Jade pieces found in tombs can also look reddish-brown on the surface and along cracks penetrating the interior.

Black or Gray Jade: Black jade, which is mined in Wyoming and Australia, is usually nephrite. Gray jade is typically jadeite and can range from dark to light in color. Black and gray jade are relative new-comers to jade jewelry and have become quite popular in the past twenty years.

White jadeite: This can range from a translucent gray-white to an opaque, milky white. Usually it's accompanied by other jade colors.

White Nephrite: Normally, this jade is not a true white. It's usually grayish. When it has a yellowish cast, it is sometimes referred to as **"mutton-fat" jade**. This jade is used to make attractive carvings.

For additional information, consult *Jade* by Roger Keverne, *Jade, Stone of Heaven* by Richard Gump, and *Jade for You* by John Ng and Edmond Root. The last two books are currently out of print but may be found in libraries or used bookstores.

Jadeite Colors

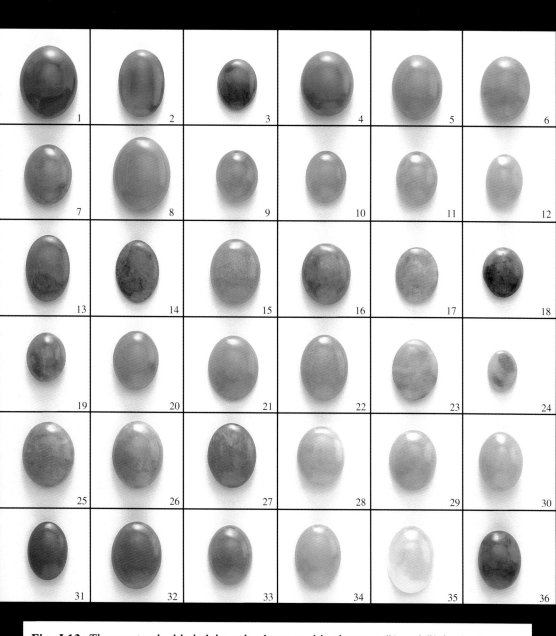

Fig. J.13 The most valuable jadeite cabochons on this chart are #1 and #2 in the top row. Number 1 is the most expensive, even though #2 photographed better in the photo. The most valuable lavender cab is #25. In the bottom row, #31 is the most valuable color. Note: the actual colors of these stones may be slightly different than shown. The printing and developing processes usually alter the true color of gems in photographs. *Chart and stones courtesy Mason-Kay; photos by Richard Rubins.*

Lapis Lazuli (a rock composed of lazurite and some calcite, pyrite and other minerals)

9th wedding anniversary stone

For over 5000 years, lapis lazuli (lapis) has been mined in Northeastern Afghanistan. This is still the world's most important source both in terms of quality and quantity. During the 1980's, Afghan rebels sold a great deal of lapis in order to get cash for weapons. They used these against the Russian troops who invaded their country. As a result, the price of lapis dropped.

The name *lapis lazuli* is from the Latin word for stone, *lapis,* and the Persian *lazhward* meaning blue. Up until the Middle Ages, lapis was called *sapphirus*, which also means blue. In ancient texts such as the Bible, the term sapphire most likely refers to lapis lazuli.

The Ancient Egyptians, Greeks and Romans not only used lapis for adornment, they ground it up to make eye shadow, medicine and a pigment called ultramarine, which was used in many of the world's famous paintings. Today lapis is one of the most popular stones for men's jewelry and it is used to make beads, watch dials, boxes, figurines and other decorative articles.

The most valued lapis has a natural, even, deep violet-blue color that is free of white calcite veining. It also has a high polish and a bit of pyrite. Dyed lapis is the least valuable type. Dye is used to improve the color and to hide white calcite. Often, the dye is not very stable and may rub off on your skin. A wax coating is commonly used to seal in the dye and to make the polish look better. It's not always possible for a salesperson to know if lapis has been dyed. However, if they claim the color is natural and the stone is untreated, have them write this on the receipt. Generally, most lapis beads are dyed. Dye can frequently be detected by rubbing the stone with cotton dipped in finger-nail polish remover or alcohol. Never do this in a conspicuous spot and always get permission first.

The second most important source of lapis is Chile. However, Chilean lapis tends to contain a lot of white calcite and the color can be relatively light. Consequently it is often dyed. German and Swiss lapis are not lapis lazuli. They're blue dyed jasper, the most widely used lapis imitation.

Fig. L.1 Lapis lazuli. The cabochon with the teardrop shape has the best depth of color.

Fig. L.2 Lapis lazuli earrings made by Richard Kimball. *Photo by Steve Ramsey.*

Malachite (Cu₂CO₃OH₂) a hydrated copper carbonate; a common ore of copper

As early as 3000 BC, malachite was recovered from the copper mines of Egypt and Israel. Besides being used for jewelry, charms and ornaments, it was ground into powder and worn as eye make-up. The same powdered pigment is used by painters under the name of mountain green.

Malachite is usually banded with differing shades of green in agate-like patterns. It's beautiful, yet low-priced. You should be able to find, for example, a nice-quality 12 x 10 mm cabochon for less than $15. Reasonably-priced beads, figurines, mosaics, boxes and other decorative objects are also available. Often, malachite is banded and intermixed with other copper minerals such as blue azurite. In this case, the resulting material is called **azurmalachite**.

Due to its perfect cleavage and very low hardness (3.5–4), malachite can easily break and scratch. It's also sensitive to heat, acids and ammonia. Sometimes, malachite is impregnated with wax or epoxy to improve the polish and hide small cracks. Never clean it ultrasonically; just wipe it with lukewarm, soapy water and rinse.

Currently, Zaire is the major producer of malachite. Other sources include Russia, Zambia, Namibia, Arizona, New Mexico and Australia.

Fig. Ma.1 Azurmalachite earrings. *Design by Lori Braun; jewelry & photo copyright by Murphy Design.*

Fig. Ma.2 Malachite carving.

Moonstone & Some Other Feldspars (A group of closely related minerals)
Moonstone—Alternate birthstone for June

Over half of the earth's crust is composed of minerals from the feldspar group and most are not gemstones. All varieties require special care since they can be easily cleaved (split) and chipped. In fact, "feldspar" is derived from "field" and "spar," a word that refers to any shiny rock that cleaves easily. Listed below are optical and physical properties of feldspars.

Hardness: 6– 6.5	**Toughness:** Poor	**Optic Character:** DR, biaxial; AGG reaction common
RI: 1.52–1.54 (moonstone & amazonite); 1.54–1.55 (oligoclase); 1.56–1.57 (labradorite)		
SG: 2.54–2.63 (moonstone & amazonite); 2.62–2.65 (oligoclase); 2.69– 2.72 (labradorite)		
Crystal System: Monoclinic (moonstone); triclinic (amazonite, oligoclase and labradorite)		
Pleochroism: Usually none, but some transparent types may show weak to moderate pleochroism		
Cleavage: Perfect and easy in two directions; parting is also common		
Stability to heat: May crack or cleave; amazonite may also lose color		
Care tips: Avoid ultrasonics, steamers, heat, acids & rough handling. Warm, soapy water is safe.		
Treatments: Normally none, except for amazonite which may be waxed and/or irradiated.		

MOONSTONE: In India, people once believed that moonstone was solidified moonlight. It is supposed to bring good fortune and help you foretell future events. Moonstones are noted for a floating light effect and sheen called **adularescence**, which has been compared to the light of the moon. This phenomenon results from alternating layers of two kinds of feldspar (usually orthoclase and albite) which cause light to scatter. High moonstone cabochons may resemble cat's-eye gems due to the concentration of light along the top of the stone.

Moonstone is typically white, colorless or light grayish blue, but it may also be yellow, orange, brown, blue or green. It ranges from near transparent to almost opaque. The most valued stones are blue and near transparent—sometimes $100 a carat. Translucent white stones can cost less than $5 per carat. Major sources are Sri Lanka, Burma and India.

LABRADORITE: This name most often refers to a dark, opaque feldspar, first found in Labrador, that displays a flash of color(s) when viewed at certain angles. This optical effect, called **labradorescence**, is typically bright blue, but it can also be green, yellow, orange or rarely purple. In a more general sense, "labradorite" includes some feldspars which are more transparent. Examples would be Oregon sunstone and **rainbow** labradorite, a nearly transparent, colorless stone with multicolored labradorescence. This labradorite is often sold as **rainbow moonstone**. **Spectrolite** is a trade name for a labradorite from Finland with strong, distinctive color flashes.

YELLOW ORTHOCLASE: A collector stone, this is usually transparent and faceted.

SUNSTONE: There are two main types of sunstone. The best known, aventurine feldspar (oligoclase), is opaque and has glittery red or golden inclusions. Another transparent type, labradorite, is orange, yellow, red or colorless. It is the state gem of Oregon.

AMAZONITE (Amazon Stone): A bluish-green variety, this is sometimes sold as "Pikes Peak jade" in Colorado. It's also found in Virginia, India, Russia and Africa.

Fig. Fe.1 Five moonstones, *Brooch from Paula Crevoshay; photo by Azad.*

Fig. Fe.2 Yellow orthoclase. *Photo Robert Weldon.*

Fig. Fe.3 Oligoclase sunstone

Fig. Fe.4 Amazonite

Fig. Fe.5 Labradorite sunstone. State gem of Oregon.

Fig. Fe.6 Labradorite

Fig. Fe.7 Rainbow labradorite

Fig. Fe.8 Spectrolite from Tom DeGasperis. *Photo by Shelly Smith.*

Opal

SiO_2nH_2O—Silica + water, about 3 to 10% water in opals with a play-of-color
Alternate birthstone for October and 14th wedding anniversary stone

Before 1829, opals were said to bring good fortune because they possessed the colors and powers of all gemstones. Then Sir Walter Scott published his novel *Anne of Gerstein*. In it, one of the characters wore a gorgeous opal that would change color depending on her mood. One day when a few drops of holy water were sprinkled on the opal, she fainted and died shortly thereafter. Convinced that this meant opals were unlucky, readers stopped buying the gem. Within a year of the novel's publication, the opal market had crashed and prices were down about 50%. The fact that opals occasionally crack when cut and set reinforced this new superstition. Queen Victoria helped the stone regain its popularity. She wore it during her reign and she gave opal jewelry to her children and friends. Thanks to opal finds in Australia in the 1870's, the queen had a good selection to choose from.

The ancient Latin name for opal was *Opalus*, which was apparently derived from the Sanskrit *Upala* meaning "precious stone." The Greek word for opal, *opállios*, means "to see a change (of color)." White opal was probably first mined at Czerwenitza, Czechoslovakia (formerly Hungary). Archival evidence shows that this mine was in operation in the 14th century, but it most likely was worked much earlier. In Mexico, fire opal was probably known to the Aztecs as early as the 13th century. The first unrecorded discovery of opal in Australia is said to be in 1849; the 1872 discovery of boulder opal in Queensland was the first recorded find. Today the greatest proportion of the world's opal comes from Australia. Opal is also found in Mexico, Brazil, the U.S., Japan and Honduras, but the finest quality is produced in Australia.

If you were to examine opal under an electron microscope at 20,000X magnification, you would see a mass of closely packed, tiny silica spheres. Opals show a **play-of-color** (a shifting of spectral colors) when the spheres are of uniform size and arranged in regular three-dimensional layers. The color or range of colors of the opal are determined by the size of the spheres. Light bends and splits as it passes through the spheres, causing spectral colors to appear at different angles. The brighter and more distinctive the play-of-color, the better the opal. Not all opals show a play-of-color. However, they do share the following properties:

RI: 1.44–1.47, Mexican opal: as low as 1.37, but usually 1.42–1.43		SG: 1.98–2.20
Hardness : 5.5–6.5	**Cleavage**: None	**Optic Character:** SR, ADR common
Pleochroism: None	**Light Stability:** Stable	**Crystal System:** Mainly amorphous
Reaction to Heat: Sudden temperature changes may cause opals to crack or craze. Over-heating can turn opals white or brownish and cause the play-of-color to disappear.		
Reaction to Chemicals: attacked by hydrofluoric acid and caustic alkalies		
Toughness: Very poor to fair depending on source and type of opal. Dealers usually keep their opals for a period of time to verify they are not susceptible to crazing, a network of fine cracks.		
Care Tips: Avoid ultrasonics, steamers, heat & chemicals, Do not immerse assembled opals in water.		
Treatments: Often impregnated with oil, wax, plastic or smoke to improve play of color, disguise cracks, increase durability and/or simulate black opal. Matrix opal is commonly dyed to simulate black opal.		

Fig. Op.1 White opal pendant. *Design, cutting and photography by Paul B. Downing.*

Fig. Op.2 An early 20th century, black opal ring. The intensity of the red is exceptional. *Opal ring from Port Royal Antique Jewelry; photo by Harold & Erica Van Pelt.*

Fig. Op.3 Fire opal ring. *Ring created by Rox Designs; photo by John Wallace.*

Fig. Op.4 Boulder opal earrings. These opals are worth more as a matched pair than if they were sold individually. *Port Royal Antique Jewelry; photo by Harold & Erica Van Pelt.*

Opal Varieties, Types and Trade Names

COMMON OPAL and **POTCH**: Opal with **no** play-of-color and a translucent to opaque transparency. It occurs in various body colors and is generally of little value. Opal with a play-of-color, the most popular kind, is called **precious opal** by many opal dealers. Red and orange Mexican opal is commonly called **fire opal** even if it has no play-of-color.

LIGHT OPAL (includes white opal, grey opal, crystal and jelly opal): Opal with a play-of-color and a light body color. **White opal** is the most common type. It typically has an off-white background color and can be translucent to opaque. Milky white stones with little play-of-color are used in budget-priced jewelry. White opals with a brilliant play-of-color can retail for a few hundred dollars per carat. When an opal has a high transparency, a near colorless body color and a distinct play-of-color, then it is called a **crystal opal**. This is the most valued light opal. In its highest qualities, it can cost more than $2500 a carat retail. A translucent opal with a play of color is sometimes called a **semi-crystal opal**. **Jelly opal** or **water opal** is near transparent to translucent and shows either an indistinct play-of-color or none at all. You can buy it for as little as $5 a carat. Better qualities may sell for $100 to $200 per carat.

BLACK (DARK) OPAL (includes black opal, semi-black opal, black crystal opal): "**Black opal**" is often used as a generic term for any opal which has a play-of-color against a dark background. In a more strict usage, black opals have a play-of-color against a black or very dark background. If the background is mid-gray to dark, the stone is classified as a **semi-black opal**. If the stone is transparent to semi-transparent and dark with a play-of-color, the stone is a **black crystal opal**.

The dividing lines between black, semi-black and gray opals can vary from one dealer to another. You need to look at comparison stones to understand the various depths of body colors and even then it can be hard to distinguish between some black and semi-black opals.

When black opal was discovered in Australia in 1903, it was not well accepted. Many people assumed that it was treated opal or white opal cemented to black onyx. Some jewelers considered it valueless. Today top-grade black opal can sell for $15,000 a carat. Some exceptional stones have even sold for over $20,000 a carat.

BOULDER OPAL: Opal that is still attached to the rock (usually ironstone) in which it is found. This opal is found in boulders whose cracks and spaces have been infiltrated with opal. Boulder opal, which can resemble either light or dark opal, is typically cut in irregular shapes. Gem quality boulder opal may sell for $5000 to $50,000 dollars per piece, but you can get attractive stones for a few hundred dollars. For people who cannot afford a colorful black opal, boulder opal can be a good alternative. It costs less because the stone is not solid opal. It is a layer of opal naturally adhered to a rock backing. Boulder opal is mined in Queensland, Australia.

MATRIX OPAL or **OPAL-IN-MATRIX:** Stones with lines or spots of opal randomly scattered (mixed) throughout the **matrix** (host rock—the rock in which a mineral, fossil or pebble is found). There are several types found in the market. The most common is a porous opal from Andamooka, Australia, which is often dyed black to simulate black opal. **Yowah opal**, another type of matrix opal, is completely natural and is mined in Yowah, South Queensland. The patches and lines of opal in its ironstone matrix often form distinctive patterns. Matrix opal normally sells for much less than boulder opal.

FIRE OPAL: A transparent to translucent opal with a red, orange, yellow or brownish body color both with or without a play-of-color. Mexico is the main source. Since consumers often assume

Fig. Op.5 Colorful examples of common opal: Source, top left to right—Oregon, Africa, Nevada, Africa, Oregon; bottom left to right—Mexico, Oregon, Mexico, Mexico, Peru.

Fig. Op.6 Light-colored boulder opal pendant.

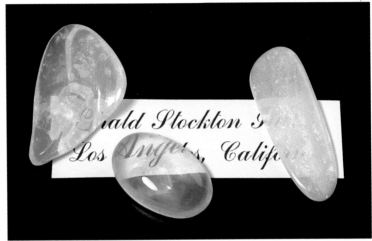

Fig. Op.7 Left to right: a crystal shell opal (ancient shell replaced by opal), a crystal opal from Lightning Ridge, and a semi-crystal opal.

Fig. Op.8 Yowah opal ring. *Rox Designs; photo by John Wallace.*

Fig. Op.9 White opal squares set in a brooch. *Designed, constructed and photographed by The Diamond Dove, Inc.*

that a fire opal is any opal with a lot of red play-of-color, some trade members think it would be better to simply call it orange or red opal, depending on its color. The most valued fire opal is reddish orange, transparent, and has a play-of-color within the stone. This quality can retail for as much as $300 per carat. Translucent stones that are yellowish or brownish may sell for around $5 per carat.

Treatments, Assembled Stones, Etc.

Opal is sometimes impregnated with oil, wax or plastic to improve the play-of-color and to prevent or disguise cracking. The plastic is stable, but the oil and wax isn't. There are various techniques for creating the appearance of black opal. These include smoke impregnation, backing with black or colored paint, and treatment with dye, silver nitrate or sugar carbonized by acid. One should avoid repolishing or applying solvents to treated opal.

If you'd like a stone with a black-opal look at an inexpensive price, consider getting an opal doublet or triplet. An **opal doublet** (also called **doublet opal**) is a thin slice of opal cemented usually with black glue to another material such as potch opal, chalcedony or glass. If this doublet also has a protective top of colorless quartz or glass, then it is called an **opal triplet** or a **triplet opal**. Doublets are normally more expensive than triplets because more opal is used. Do not confuse these assembled stones with boulder opal, which has a naturally attached backing. Often you can detect the man-made stones by looking at them from the side. A doublet typically has a straight separation line whereas a boulder opal has a crooked one. There are also fake opal stones. One is called **Slocum Stone** and another **Opalite**. Hong Kong is a major producer of imitation opal. Synthetic opal is grown in Japan and Russia.

Factors Which Affect Opal Value

Opal type: Solid black opal is more expensive than boulder opal if similar qualities and colors of each category are compared. Matrix opals and assembled stones are the least expensive types. There's a great difference in price between a natural and an assembled opal of similar appearance, so it's important to have salespeople identify the type of opal both verbally and on the receipt.

Body Tone: (The darkness or lightness of the background color): Black opal is more expensive than light opal of like quality. With black and boulder opal, generally the darker the background the more valuable the stone is. When determining body tone, look at the top of the stone.

Brilliance: The overall brightness and intensity of the play-of-color. The more brilliant the flashes of color, the better the stone. Examine brilliance both under a consistent light source and away from it. Stones that maintain their brightness away from light are the most highly valued. Brilliance is one of the most important value factors.

Play-of-Color: The dominant color(s) and the combination of colors are both important. Intense red is the most rare and therefore the most prized color. In terms of value, it's followed by orange, green and blue, the most plentiful color. The way in which different color combinations are priced can vary from one dealer to another. Any type of play-of-color can be desirable, as long as the colors are intense and not dull when viewed face up.

Fig. Op.10 This distinctive black opal is called the "globe opal" because its patterns resemble the oceans and continents. *Courtesy Port Royal Antique Jewelry; photo by Harold & Erica Van Pelt.*

Fig. Op.11 A black opal with exceptional brilliance and a high intensity of color. Compare it to the opal in the preceding photo. *Port Royal Antique Jewelry; photo Harold & Erica Van Pelt.*

Fig. Op.12 Boulder opal with matrix showing. *Courtesy Proprioro; TKO Studios.*

Fig. Op.13 A black opal with a predominantly red color. This is a rare, collector-quality opal. *Port Royal Antique Jewelry; photo by Harold & Erica Van Pelt.*

Fig. Op.14 A low-quality milky white opal.

Fig. Op.15 Side view of an opal doublet.

Fig. Op.16 Face-up view of same doublet.

Color Pattern: The diffracted colors in opals are displayed in various patterns: **pinfire**—small pin-point like color specks; **flashfire**—larger splashes of color, usually irregular in shape; **broad flashfire**—sheets of color normally covering a large section or all of a stone's surface; **harlequin**—square or angular patches of color set close together like a mosaic; **fancy patterns and picture stones**—unusual patterns that form pictures or resemble things such as Chinese writing, straw, flowers, cat's-eye stones, etc. Pinfire and small type patterns are generally less desirable than broad patterns or large flashes. Harlequin and distinctive fancy patterns are especially valuable.

Transparency: For light opal and fire opal, the higher the transparency, the more valuable the stone. For black opal, the opaque, blacker stones tend to be more highly valued than those with greater transparency.

Shape: The most sought-after traditional shape is a well-formed oval. It tends to bring a higher price than other shapes because it's in greater demand, it's easier to set, and valuable opal material is sacrificed when stones are cut as ovals. Many jewelers and designers, however, prefer other shapes, especially freeforms because they are more distinctive. Unusual freeforms may sell for more than ovals, especially after they are mounted.

Cut: All else being equal, domed cabochons tend to be more valued than flat ones. Excessive weight on the bottom and a thin or unsymmetrical profile can all reduce the value of an opal.

Size and Carat Weight: Stones under a carat are generally worth less per carat than larger ones. If a stone is unusually large, it may be worth less per carat than stones more suitable for general jewelry use. Boulder opals are typically priced by size rather than carat weight. The larger the opal the higher the price.

Imperfections: Opal value decreases when there are eye-visible imperfections on the top of the stone such as sand or gypsum. The larger and more noticeable they are, the greater their impact on value. Inclusions on the back of a stone have little or no effect on price unless they hurt the structural integrity of the stone. Cracks drastically reduce value. A common opal flaw is **crazing**—a thin, network of fractures that resembles a spider web. When deep, it has a serious impact on price. Opals with a high water content are the ones most subject to crazing. There are ways of concealing crazing, but no honest opal dealer would do that without disclosing it. Many dealers offer some type of guarantee against crazing that is typically valid for one year. However, this guarantee is not against cracks, which are usually the result of abuse or poor setting skills. To prevent crazing in dry environments such as safe deposit boxes, some dealers store their opals in distilled water. Others say this is unnecessary. At any rate, water does not hurt the opal. Opals sometimes have pattern lines which look like cracks but aren't. These lines are natural changes in the pattern of an opal and are not regarded as flaws.

Since opals are relatively soft and fragile, they require special care. Avoid heat and sudden changes of temperature. Do not wear them while sunbathing or set them on a sunny window sill or under hot lights. Do not clean them in ultrasonics. Instead, wash them in lukewarm water with a mild soap and soft cloth. (Opal doublets and triplets, however, should not be immersed in water.) Store opal jewelry separately in cloth pouches. Take rings off when doing housework and engaging in sports. With proper care, opals can give you a lifetime of enjoyment.

Two good sources for more information on opal evaluation are *Australian Precious Opal* by Andrew Cody and *Opal Identification and Value* by Paul Downing.

Fig. Op.17 Pinfire pattern in a boulder opal pendant. *Port Royal Antique Jewelry; photo by Harold & Erica Van Pelt.*

Fig. Op.18 An unusual cat's eye pattern in a black opal. *Port Royal Antique Jewelry; photo by Harold & Erica Van Pelt.*

Fig. Op.19 A rare Australian black opal with a play of color that is mostly red, pink and orange. *Port Royal Antique Jewelry; photo by Harold & Erica Van Pelt.*

Fig. Op.20 A badly crazed white opal.

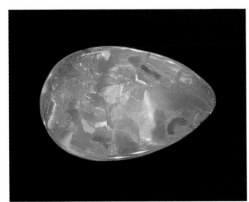

Fig. Op. 21 A black opal with a flashfire pattern and internal crazing. *Port Royal Antique Jewelry; photo by Harold & Erica Van Pelt.*

Fig. Op.22 This black opal sold at a low price because it looked cracked. It turned out that the opal simply had pattern lines. *Port Royal Antique Jewelry; photo by Harold & Erica Van Pelt.*

Peridot (Olivine group, forsterite species) $(Mg,Fe)_2SiO_4$—Magnesium iron silicate

August birthstone, 16th wedding anniversary stone

According to legend, you will be protected from evil spirits if you wear peridot (also called **chrysolite**). This rich, yellowish-green gem has sometimes been mistaken for emerald. Many of Cleopatra's "emeralds" were probably peridots. Adding further confusion, peridot was called topaz in ancient times.

Peridot is attractive, yet affordable. You can purchase a high quality peridot for less than $150 per carat retail. The greener the stone and the better the clarity, the higher the value is. If yellow or orange colors complement your skin, then peridot jewelry should also look good on you. It is particularly flattering to people with blond or red hair.

Peridot has been mined for over 3500 years. The oldest source is St. John's Island, Egypt, in the Red Sea. Pakistan and Arizona are the main sources today. Other deposits include Myanmar, China, Brazil, Kenya and Norway. Physical and optical characteristics of peridot are given below:

RI: 1.64–1.69	SG: 3.27–3.45	Hardness: 6.5–7	Toughness: Fair to good
Pleochroism: weak	Cleavage: Indistinct	Crystal Sys: Orthorhombic	Optic Char: DR, biaxial + or -
Stability to Heat: Rapid or uneven heat can cause peridot to crack or break.			
Reaction to Chemicals: Attacked by sulfuric and HCl acid. Acid perspiration of some people over a long period may etch the surface. Jewelers should never put peridot in pickling solutions.			
Care Tips: Ultrasonics are risky; avoid steamers, acids and abrupt temperature changes.			
Treatments: normally not treated; the color is natural. Occasionally fracture-filled if fractures are present.			

Fig. P.1 Peridot and freshwater pearl pendant

Fig. P.2 Peridot ring hand-fabricated by Varna Platinum

Spodumene LiAlSi₂O₆—Lithium and aluminum silicate

KUNZITE, which is pink to purple in color, is the best-known spodumene variety. Found in California in 1902, it was named after George Frederick Kunz, a famous gemologist and former vice-president of Tiffany & Co. Some of the kunzite available today is irradiated to intensify its color. Unfortunately, the color fades over time when exposed to strong light or heat. Kunzite is typically eye-clean and low priced. You can find well-cut, light pink stones of high clarity for under $100 per carat retail. Stones with a more saturated color are available, but they can be difficult to find in North America or Europe. These stones are often reserved for buyers in Japan.

Spodumene can also be yellow to green in color. The rare emerald-green variety is called **HIDDENITE**. It was discovered in North Carolina in 1879 by William Hidden. Don't expect to find hiddenite in your local jewelry store or rock shop. The deposit is very small and production has always been sporadic. In 1904, mineralogist Max Bauer valued fine, green transparent hiddenite at $50 to $100 per carat in his book, *Precious Stones*. According to mineralogist John S. White, the North Carolina site is currently being worked, and a deep-green, 1-carat hiddenite from there is now priced at about $10,000. Some light green material from Brazil and other areas is sold as hiddenite. However, many gemologists feel it should technically be called green spodumene. They also believe that irradiated green stones do not merit being called hiddenite.

The major sources of kunzite and other spodumene varieties are Afghanistan, Madagascar, Brazil and the U.S. Physical and optical characteristics of spodumene are given below:

RI: 1.66–1.68	SG: 3.14–3.21	Hardness: 6.5–7	Monoclinic	Toughness: Poor
Trichroism: Moderate to strong		Cleavage: Perfect in two directions		DR, biaxial positive
Reaction to heat: Sensitive; kunzite fades; irradiated green spodumene fades rapidly.				
Stability to light: Kunzite fades; irradiated green spodumene fades rapidly				
Care Tips: Avoid ultrasonic cleaners, rough handling, strong light, heat and acids.				
Treatments: Kunzite—commonly heated and irradiated; Other spodumenes—occasionally irradiated				

Fig. Sp.1 Green spodumene crystal

Fig. Sp.2 Kunzite

Ruby & Sapphire (Corundum) Al_2O_3—Aluminum Oxide

Ruby—July birthstone; sapphire—September birthstone; ruby—15th & 40th anniversary stone; sapphire—5th & 45th anniversary stone.

Ruby and sapphire have a lot in common. They are the same mineral—corundum. They have the same physical characteristics. They have both been considered regal and sacred. In ancient India, the ruby was called the king of "gems." In England the ruby was used for coronation rings. Sapphires were worn by kings and queens for good luck and they were set in rings for bishops and cardinals. Their blue color symbolized heaven. The ancient Hindus thought that if they offered a ruby to the god Krishna, they would be reborn as an emperor.

Color is what distinguishes ruby from sapphire. Rubies are red and sapphires are either blue or another color such as green, orange, pink, yellow, purple, colorless or black (sapphire colors other than blue are called **fancy colors)**. It wasn't until about 1800 that ruby and sapphire were recognized as being the same mineral. Before then, red spinel and garnet were also called ruby. The name was derived from the Latin word for red, *rubeus*. "Sapphire" is from a Greek word meaning blue.

Rubies and sapphires are harder than all other gems except diamonds. Their superior hardness combined with the lack of cleavage makes them a very durable gem. It also makes them valuable for industrial purposes. They have been produced synthetically so they can serve as laser windows, tips in ball-point pins, styluses for record players and jewel bearings in watches, meters and aircraft instruments. The properties of ruby and sapphire are given below.

RI: 1.76–1.78	SG: 3.95–4.05	Hardness: 9	Crystal System: Trigonal
Cleavage: None, twinned stones may show parting			Optic Character: DR, uniaxial negative
Toughness: Excellent, except fractured or repeatedly twinned stones; may abrade easily if improperly heated			
Pleochroism: Ruby—strong purplish red and orangy red; sapphire—moderate to strong violetish blue and greenish blue; fancy-color sapphires—weak to strong dichroism			
Stability to Light: Stable except for irradiated yellow and orange sapphires, which may fade			
Care Tips: Ultrasonics and steamers are safe if stones aren't oiled, cavity filled, or heavily flawed.			
Treatments: Assume that corundum is heated unless otherwise stated. Unheated stones are available. Fracture filling with oil, epoxy or glass—common in ruby; Diffusion treatment or dyeing—sometimes done; Irradiation—sometimes done to produce yellow or orange sapphire from colorless or light yellow			

Varieties

RUBY: In 1896, German mineralogist Max Bauer wrote: *A clear transparent, and faultless ruby of a uniform deep red colour is at the present time the most valuable stone known.* Today diamonds have surpassed rubies in value, but Bauer's description of a top-quality ruby is still valid. Dealers disagree, however, on whether orangy-red rubies are better than those which are purplish-red. They would agree that a strong red fluorescence is desirable and that top-grade stones should have a minimal amount of black, gray or brown. Their color should also look good in any light. The highest percentage of stones that have met these color criteria are from the Mogok area of Myanmar (Burma). Do not assume, though, that a ruby is good quality if it originates from Mogok.

Fig. RS.1 Above: Sapphire and diamond necklace. *Photo and necklace courtesy Harry Winston, Inc.*

Fig. RS.2 Right: Thai ruby and diamond ring. *Photo and ring courtesy Color Masters Gem Corp.*

Likewise, don't assume that rubies from other localities such as Thailand, Cambodia, Vietnam, Madagascar, Sri Lanka, Tanzania and Kenya must be inferior. High-quality material has originated from all of these countries.

Large rubies have sold for as much as $200,000 per carat, but good rubies with inclusions in the 1-carat range are available for $3000-$4000 per carat. You can also find opaque rubies for as low as $10 per carat. A premium may be charged if a high-grade stone originates from Mogok or shows no evidence of heat treatment, providing it has a lab report from a respected lab. Rubies are normally heat-treated to improve color and/or clarity. Diffusion treatment, large glass fillings and red oils or dyes greatly affect value (see chapter on treatments).

SAPPHIRE: When used by itself, the term **sapphire** normally refers to the blue variety. In its highest qualities, it is more expensive than the other varieties. Top-quality Kashmir sapphires, for example, can wholesale for over $20,000 a carat (Mining in Kashmir has been extremely limited for decades). There are differences of opinion as to what is the best sapphire hue. Some say blue, others say violetish blue. Most dealers agree, however, that greenish blues are less valuable. Dealers also have different tone preferences. Some prefer medium tones of blue while others prefer medium-dark tones. Pale, blackish or grayish stones, however, cost the least. Good sapphires in the one-carat range are available for $1000 to $3000 retail. Kashmir sapphires have the highest prestige, followed by those from Burma and then Sri Lanka. Today, Madagascar is the major producer of sapphire. Thailand, Cambodia and Australia are also important sources. The lowest priced stones often come from Australia because they tend to be overly dark and have a low transparency. Sapphire is also found in India, Montana, China and various African countries. Sapphires are usually heat treated. Their outer surface is sometimes darkened by diffusion treatment, but this must always be disclosed.

PADPARADSCHA: A pinkish-orange sapphire, padparadscha is the rarest and most prized of all the fancy sapphires. Its name is believed to have come from the Sinhalese word for the lotus flower, which has a similar color. Frequently, orange sapphire is called padparadscha, but most dealers agree that both pink and orange hues must be present for a stone to be a true padparadscha; some say the color must be natural. Don't expect to find this rare gem at your local jeweler's.

PINK SAPPHIRE: Next to the padparadscha, this is the most highly prized of all the fancy sapphires. Since "pink" is a synonym of "light red" and since fine rubies cost more than sapphires, many Asian dealers prefer to call pink sapphires rubies. The jewelry trade in western countries prefers to treat the pink sapphire as a unique stone with its own merits, rather than as a second-rate ruby. Top-quality pink sapphires can cost several thousand dollars per carat.

ORANGE, PURPLE, YELLOW OR GREEN SAPPHIRE: Madagascar, East Africa, Sri Lanka, Thailand and Montana are sources of these sapphires. A high percentage of green sapphire is found in Australia. Of these four sapphire colors, orange is the most valued (if it's not-diffusion treated), green is typically the lowest priced; and yellow is usually the most readily available.

COLORLESS SAPPHIRE (WHITE SAPPHIRE): This sapphire is made by heat-treating light-colored sapphire. In recent years, white sapphire has become popular as a diamond substitute.

STAR SAPPHIRE AND STAR RUBY: Star corundum with a fine blue or red color is rare. Gray, maroon and black star stones are easier to find, and their prices can be relatively low.

More detailed information on the identification and quality analysis of corundum is available in the *Ruby, Sapphire & Emerald Buying Guide* by Renée Newman and in *Ruby & Sapphire* by Richard Hughes.

Fig. RS.3 Sapphires come in a wide range colors, as this photo shows. The dividing line between ruby and pink sapphire or reddish-orange sapphire is debatable. Three of the stones pictured would be called rubies by many dealers. Others would call them sapphires. In Asia, even the two light pink stones might be identified as rubies. *Gemstones from Cynthia Renée Co; photo by Robert Weldon.*

Fig. RS.4 Unheated Madagascar blue sapphire (5 cts) with pair of Sri Lankan pink sapphires (5 cts tw); pair of Madagascar pink sapphires (13 ct tw). *Hand-fabricated platinum rings from Cynthia Renée Co; photo by Robert Weldon.*

Fig. RS.5 Padparadscha. *Gemstone from Radiance International; photo by Robert Weldon.*

Spinel $MgAl_2O_4$—Magnesium aluminum oxide

22nd wedding anniversary stone

If you're looking for a natural gem that resembles a ruby but costs a lot less, you should consider getting a spinel. It's durable, comparatively hard and typically has a better clarity and brilliance than a ruby. Not all red spinels can pass as rubies, but many do. Some of the world's largest and most famous "rubies" are really spinels, such as the "Black Princes Ruby" and the 361-ct "Timur Ruby" in the English crown jewels. Spinel comes in other colors such as blue, pink, orange and black, but red is the most valued. Stones over ten carats are rare.

Natural spinel does not enjoy the popularity that it merits. One reason for this is that its often confused with the synthetic spinel used in inexpensive birthstone rings and costume jewelry. In addition, natural spinel is not available in mass quantities, so it's not widely known and advertised. However, custom jewelers and collectors who like unusual gems appreciate spinel.

The main sources of spinel are Myanmar (Burma) and Sri Lanka. Other localities include Thailand, Cambodia, Afghanistan, Tanzania, Russia and Vietnam. Spinel is often a by-product of the search for ruby and sapphire. Its properties are as follows:

RI: 1.71–1.73 (gem spinel)	SG: 3.57 - 3.63 (black spinel, up to 4.0)		Crystal Sys: Cubic
Cleavage: Poorly developed	Hardness: 8	Toughness: Good	Optic Character: SR
Stability to Light: Stable	Light colored stones may fade under intense heat.		Pleochroism: None
Care Tips: Ultrasonics and steamers are usually safe		Reaction to Chemicals: none	
Treatments: Normally none. The colors are natural.			

Varieties

RED SPINEL: The most valuable red spinels resemble a high-quality ruby. A one-carat stone can retail for over $1000. In sizes above five carats they may sell for over $3000 per carat. Low-quality brownish stones are available for under $100 a carat.

PINK SPINEL: This resembles pink sapphire but costs about one-fourth to one-half the price.

ORANGE SPINEL: Its color range is from yellow-orange to red-orange. This spinel is sometimes called **flame spinel**. Formerly it was called **rubicelle**.

BLUE SPINEL: Fine blue colors are rare and can retail for over $2000 per carat. This spinel tends to be grayish or very dark. In an attempt to lighten the color, stones are often cut shallow. Blue spinel is mined in Sri Lanka and Myanmar.

BLACK SPINEL: This spinel is opaque and rarely seen in jewelry.

COLOR-CHANGE SPINEL: A rare stone, it's grayish-blue in daylight and purplish under incandescent light-bulbs.

STAR SPINEL: This is rare and generally gray, blue or black with 4 or 6 rays.

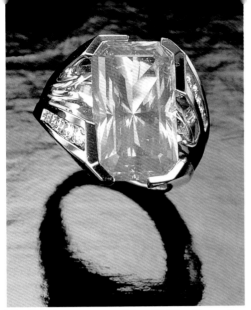

Fig. S.1 A very rare and fine 10.68-ct Tanzanian pink spinel. *Gem from Cynthia Renée Co.; ring by Paul Klecka; photo by Robert Weldon.*

Fig. S.2 Spinels in a pendant by Gary Dulac. *Photo copyright 1994 by Azad.*

Fig. S.3 Burmese red spinel and spinel crystals. *Gems from Cynthia Renée Co; photo by Robert Weldon.*

Fig. S.4 Spinel ring created and photographed by LInda Quinn.

Fig. S.5 Blue spinel ring from Cynthia Renée Co. *Photo by Robert Weldon.*

Tanzanite & Other Zoisites $Ca_3Al_3(SiO_4)_3(OH)$—Calcium aluminum hydroxysilicate

Tanzanite—24th wedding anniversary stone

No history, lore or poetry was needed for tanzanite to become one of the most popular gems on the market. You just look at it and fall in love with it. From one angle it may display a rich blue color, from another it can look purple. Along with the blue and purple, there may be flashes of red, green, yellow, orange or brown. What's more, tanzanite can appear one color indoors and another outdoors. A high clarity and transparency add to its beauty.

Tanzanite was discovered in the 1960's in the foothills of Africa's Mt. Kilimanjaro. Later, Henry Platt, vice-president and director of Tiffany's, named the stone after its country of origin, Tanzania. Some mineralogists feel that the term "tanzanite" should be restricted to transparent zoisites that range in color from blue to violet to purple in color. Other colors such as green, yellow and pink are to be called by their mineralogical name **zoisite**. But since "tanzanite" sounds more exotic and appealing, some dealers tend to use it for all transparent zoisites. However, as with sapphire, the unmodified "tanzanite" refers to the blue or violet variety, whereas other colors must be specified, e.g. yellow tanzanite. This practice allows dealers to distinguish between the transparent and non-transparent green varieties. In the marketplace, for example, green tanzanite is transparent green zoisite whereas green zoisite is typically the non-transparent variety used for carvings. Some European mineralogists call the green, non-transparent type, **anyolite**. Listed below are the properties of zoisite.

RI: 1.69–1.70	SG: 3.20–3.40	Hardness: 6–7	Crystal System: Orthorhombic
Cleavage: Perfect in one direction		**Optic Character:** DR, biaxial positive	
Toughness: Fair to poor; tanzanite's perfect cleavage makes it vulnerable to bumps and knocks.			
Pleochroism: Very strong; in tanzanite, the trichroism is blue, purple, and green, yellow or brown.			
Reaction to Chemicals: Attacked by hydrochloric and hydrofluoric acid			
Stability to Light: Stable; the colors resulting from heat treatment are permanent.			
Care Tips: Avoid ultrasonics, steamers, abrupt temperature changes and rough handling			
Treatments: Almost all tanzanite is heated to produce non-brownish tanzanite colors.			

TANZANITE: Some dealers feel that a deep blue with a faint purple secondary color is the most desirable. Others prefer an equal mix of blue and purple. Most dealers would agree, though, that blue stones are worth more than those which are purple. Light lavender stones are priced the lowest. You can find large, high-quality, deep-blue tanzanites with purple overtones for less than $1200 per carat retail. Attractive light lavender tanzanite is available for less than $400 per carat retail. Prices vary depending on size, quality and availability. Most tanzanite is heat-treated to intensify the color and/or eliminate brown, gray or green.

THULITE: This semi-translucent pink zoisite, often mottled with gray, is used for cabochons or carvings. Also called **rosaline**, thulite is found in Norway, Austria, Italy, Australia and the U.S.

GREEN, YELLOW, ORANGE or PINK TRANSPARENT ZOISITE: It may be hard to find these varieties. Their prices are usually in the same range as those of blue or purple tanzanite.

GREEN ZOISITE: Often found with ruby, this translucent to opaque zoisite is frequently carved.

Fig. Tz.1 Five zoisites viewed under incandescent light bulbs. It's unusual for a tanzanite to remain as blue as the one in the upper right-hand corner in this type of lighting. It would normally become purplish.

Fig. Tz.2 Green zoisite carving

Center right: **Fig. Tz.3** Tanzanite. *Jewelry and photo from Robert Trisko Jewelry Sculptures.*

Bottom right: **Fig. Tz.4** Tanzanite ring by Proprioro. *Photo by TKO Studios.*

Topaz $Al_2(F,OH)_2SiO4$—aluminum fluorohydroxysilicate

November birthstone, imperial topaz—23rd wedding anniversary stone

Most topaz is light brown when mined and then turns colorless after exposure to light or low heat. Otherwise it tends to be pale blue. That's why yellow, orange and pink topaz are highly regarded. Good brilliance and hardness also add to their value. High-quality, yellow-orange topaz, for example, may cost several hundred dollars per carat whereas citrine quartz of similar color and quality may sell for less than $35 a carat. Due to the price difference, some sellers call citrine quartz, which is widely available, "quartz topaz" or even "topaz" to make it sound more expensive. Prior to the 18th century, all yellow stones and some green ones were usually called "topaz." Even today, some miners refer to almost any yellow stone as a topaz. Therefore, when buying topaz, ask the seller to specify on the receipt that it is genuine topaz and not quartz or another gemstone.

The world's largest producer of topaz is the state of Minas Gerais in Brazil. For almost 300 years, its Ouro Preto district has supplied the world with yellow, orange and pink topaz. Other sources include the U.S., Pakistan, Sri Lanka, Russia, Germany, Mexico, Australia and Myanmar. Crystals weighing several kilos are common. The properties of topaz are as follows:

RI: 1.61–1.64	SG: 3.50–3.57	Hardness: 8	Crystal System: Orthorhombic
Cleavage: Perfect in one direction		Optic Character: DR, biaxial positive	
Pleochroism: Weak to distinct trichroism		Reaction to Chemicals: Affected very slightly	
Toughness: Poor. Because of its perfect cleavage, stones can easily break, chip or form straight cracks when dropped or knocked. Topaz requires special care when being set.			
Stability to Light: Natural brownish topaz may fade, especially some from Mexico, Utah and Siberia. Yellow non-irradiated stones from Brazil and pink or blue ones are generally stable.			
Care Tips: Avoid ultrasonics, steamers, strong heat, rough handling and rapid cooling or heating			
Treatments: Blue is usually irradiated & heated; pink & red is usually heated; green is diffusion treated.			

Varieties

PINK to RED TOPAZ: Top-grade red or strong pink topaz is the most valuable type of topaz. The redder and more saturated the color, the rarer and more costly the stone. Natural-color stones, which generally come from Pakistan, can sell for much more than those which are treated. Most pink topaz is heated brownish-yellow topaz from Brazil.

GOLDEN YELLOW to ORANGE TOPAZ: When this variety is intensely colored and has reddish or pink overtones, it is called **imperial topaz** and can retail from about $200 to over $2000 per carat. Stones that lack pink highlights or have a low color saturation are less valuable.

BLUE to GREEN TOPAZ: Produced by irradiating and then heating certain colorless material, blue topaz can look like fine aquamarine, but most is a stronger blue and looks less natural. Ever since the market was flooded with this topaz, its price has dropped to levels below $20 a carat. Topaz with medium to dark green colors does not occur naturally; it's diffusion treated.

COLORLESS TOPAZ: Used to simulate diamonds, this is the cheapest and most plentiful topaz.

Fig. Tp.1 Blue topaz pendant created and photographed by Linda Quinn

Fig. Tp.2 Suite of imperial topaz from Cynthia Renée Co. *Photo by Robert Weldon.*

Fig. Tp. 3 Imperial topaz ring by Cheri Del Santo. *Topaz from Cynthia Renée Co.; photo by Robert Weldon.*

Fig. Tp.4 Pink topaz. *Stone from Manoel Bernardes Ltd. Photo by Robert Weldon.*

Fig. Tp. 5 Colorless topaz with an unusual inclusion

Fig. Tp.6 Brown topaz. The color-zoned stone on the left is light brown, colorless and gray.

Tourmaline (a group of mineral species)

Alternate birthstone for October and 8th wedding anniversary stone

No other gemstone offers buyers a wider variety of colors than tourmaline. Besides being found in every color of the rainbow, tourmaline may also be multicolored in one piece.

It wasn't until the early 18th century that tourmaline was recognized as a distinct gemstone. Up to that time, the red and green varieties were often classified as a type of ruby or emerald. Then it was discovered that tourmaline possessed curious properties. When heated or pressed at one end, it became electrically charged; it could attract and repel light-weight, non-metallic materials like ashes, dust and small bits of paper. In 1768, Linnaeus, a Swedish naturalist, suggested that green tourmaline was related to **schorl**, the black species of tourmaline which had been known for almost two centuries in Europe. The origin of "tourmaline" is uncertain. According to *Gems* by Robert Webster, it originated from the Sinhalese *turmali*, a name applied by the local jewelers to yellow zircon. Supposedly, a parcel of tourmaline was sent by mistake under this name to stone dealers in Amsterdam in 1703, and the name may have stuck.

Tourmaline has been found in significant quantities in Brazil, California, Maine, Pakistan, Afghanistan, East Africa, Madagascar, Sri Lanka and the Soviet Union. Its properties are below:

RI: 1.62–1.65	SG: 3.00–3.26		Hardness: 7–7.5	Cleavage: None
Crystal System: Hexagonal (Trigonal)		**Optic Character:** DR, uniaxial negative		
Toughness: Fair; heat-treated stones may be more fragile than untreated stones				
Pleochroism: Moderate to strong, usually light and dark tones of the same body color				
Reaction to Heat: Strong heat may cause irradiated stones to fade.				
Stability to Light: Normally stable, but some irradiated stones may fade with prolonged exposure.				
Care tips: Ultrasonics are risky. Avoid sudden temperature changes in order to prevent fracturing.				
Treatments: Heating—common; irradiation—common in red, pink & purple; fracture filling—sometimes				

Varieties and Species:

GREEN TOURMALINE: This variety is plentiful and comes in a wide range of shades. It tends to have a strong green dichroism that makes one direction of the stone (the optic axis) appear very dark and non-transparent. To lighten and improve the color, green tourmaline is commonly heat-treated. Stones that are brownish, blackish and yellowish are the least expensive. Those with an intense natural green color resembling a good emerald cost the most.

Top-color green tourmalines are found in East Africa and are typically colored by chromium. As a result, they are called **chrome tourmalines**. Not all stones sold as "chrome tourmaline" contain chromium. To test for chromium content, some dealers look at the tourmaline through a special color filter called a Chelsea filter. The stone will look reddish or pinkish instead of green if it contains chromium. Eye-clean green tourmaline is readily available. Therefore, good-quality stones are expected to have a high clarity. Top quality chrome tourmaline can retail for as much as $2000 per carat. Most green tourmaline, however, is quite affordable, with retail prices ranging from about $20 in very low qualities to $500 per carat in better stones.

Fig. Tm.1 Indicolite ring by Richard Kimball. *Photo by Steve Ramsey.*

Fig. Tm.2 Green-tourmaline slide pedant made and photographed by Linda Quinn

Fig. Tm.3 Red tourmaline ring by Richard Kimball. *Photo by Steve Ramsey.*

Fig. Tm.4 Well-matched bi-color tourmaline ring & cuff-links. *Jewelry by Cynthia Renée Co.; photo Robert Weldon*

Fig. Tm.5 Carved portrait in a slice of a watermelon tourmaline crystal.

Fig. Tm.6 Black tourmaline (schorl)

PINK or RED TOURMALINE: The discovery of pink tourmaline in southern California in 1898 helped popularize this stone. Red and pink tourmaline are also mined in Afghanistan, Brazil, Nigeria and Madagascar. **RUBELLITE** is a trade name applied to tourmaline that is red in both daylight and incandescent light. (Tourmalines that are red often turn brownish under incandescent light bulbs, and this is undesirable.) Many sellers apply the term "rubellite" to any tourmaline that is strong pink or red. But no matter which name is used, tourmalines that are pink or that look brownish-red under incandescent light should sell for less than pure-red rubellites, all other factors being equal. High quality red rubellite in the 1–10 ct range retails for about $300–$800 a carat.

Pink and red tourmalines are commonly irradiated to intensify their color. The stones are not radioactive and the color is relatively stable. However, strong heat like that from a display window or a jeweler's torch can cause the color to fade. The color will return if the stone is irradiated again. Sometimes rubellite is treated with fillers to improve its clarity. Even when treated, you should expect it to have a lower clarity than other transparent tourmalines.

BLUE TOURMALINE (INDICOLITE or INDIGOLITE): Indicolite comes in various shades of blue, but frequently, it's a dark greenish or grayish blue. The color is often lightened with heat treatment. A brighter turquoise-blue material has been found in Northeastern Brazil in the state of Paraíba. It's called **Paraíba tourmaline** and is the rarest and most expensive tourmaline. In its finest qualities, it has wholesaled for over $10,000 per carat. Paraíba tourmaline can also have an intense green or violet color. Don't expect to find it in your local jewelry store; it's rare and highly coveted. Indicolite costs less, ranging in price from about $50 to $1000 retail per carat for sizes above a carat.

YELLOW, ORANGE, BROWN or GOLDEN TOURMALINE: Yellow and orange tourmaline occur naturally but are sometimes produced by irradiating light yellow or green tourmaline. Heat can cause the resulting color to fade. The orange and yellow stones above a carat may retail for about $30 to $500 per carat. Brown tourmaline, tends to be less expensive.

COLORLESS OR WHITE TOURMALINE: This tourmaline occurs naturally in the same areas as pink tourmaline. It can also be produced by heating light pink tourmaline.

BLACK TOURMALINE (Mineralogical name **SCHORL**): This is a very common opaque stone which was widely used for mourning jewelry during the Victorian era in Britain. Today it's occasionally used instead of jet or chalcedony in very inexpensive jewelry.

BICOLORED or MULTICOLORED TOURMALINE: The pink and green variety is the most common type, but stones can also be pink and colorless or blue and green. Some stones have more than two colors. The most valued stones have distinct saturated colors with sharp boundaries and no fractures. Green and pink slices of crystal tourmaline that have concentric color banding are called **watermelon tourmaline**. It retails for about $30 to $800 per carat.

CAT'S-EYE TOURMALINE: This is found in a variety of colors but pink and green are less difficult to find than red or blue colors. Cat's-eye tourmaline is occasionally treated with epoxy fillers to improve transparency and seal the tubes causing the cat's-eye. The fillers prevent dirt from entering the tubes. Retail prices range from about $30 to $700 per carat.

COLOR-CHANGE TOURMALINE: In daylight, this tourmaline may look yellowish to brownish green whereas under incandescent light it appears orangy red. Color-change tourmaline is rare and considered a collector's item.

Fig. Tm.7 Paraiba tourmaline from Gary Dulac. *Photo Azad.*

Fig. Tm.8 Tourmalines from Afghanistan hand cut by Clay Zava of David Clay Co. *Photo by Weldon.*

Fig. Tm.9 Cat's-eye tourmalines

Fig. Tm.10 Blue-green tourmaline with red tourmaline side stones. *Jewelry by Cynthia Renée Co.; photo by Robert Weldon.*

Fig. Tm.11 Pinkish-orange tourmaline ring created and photographed by Linda Quinn.

Turquoise $CuAl_6(PO_4)_4(OH)8 \cdot 5H_2O$—hydrated copper aluminum phosphate

December birthstone and 11th wedding anniversary stone

If you go on a tour of Arizona or New Mexico, you'll no doubt see Indians selling turquoise jewelry. On the back of it, there may be a stamp saying "Made in Taiwan." Unfortunately, a glut of cheap turquoise jewelry has lowered the prestige and value of what was for centuries a highly esteemed gem. Turquoise was admired by the ancient Egyptians for its distinctive color. It is the national gemstone of Iran (Persia), where it has decorated thrones and the attire of high officials. In Tibet, it has had a role comparable to that of jade in China. To the Aztecs, turquoise was a commodity more valuable than gold. According to the 17th century book *Gemmarum et Lapidum Historia* by Anselmus de Boot, turquoise was so highly regarded by European men, that no man considered his hand to be well adorned unless he wore a fine turquoise.

The best turquoise occurs in northeast Iran near Nishapur, where it has been mined for over 3000 years. The material there is typically more stable and blue than that of other sources—China, Mexico, the Sinai Peninsula and Southwestern USA, the main producer. Persian turquoise made its way to Europe via Turkey, which is probably why by the 13th century, the French were calling it *pierre turquoise—Turkish stone*. The properties of turquoise are given below:

RI: 1.61–1.65	SG: Usually 2.60– 2.85	Hardness: 5–6	Toughness: Good to poor
Cleavage: None	Pleochroism: Weak	Crystal Sys: Triclinic	Optic Char: AGG (DR)

Reaction to Chemicals: May be discolored by perspiration, perfume, hair-spray, cosmetics, lotions, heavy liquids, soap and ultrasonic cleaning solutions. It dissolves very slowly in HCL.
Reaction to Heat: Can fracture, shatter, crackle and discolor
Stability to Light: Untreated material may fade or discolor
Care Tips: Avoid ultrasonics, steamers, chemicals and heat. Clean with warm soapy water.
Treatments: Epoxy, wax or plastic impregnation, sometimes with a colorant: common

As this chart shows, natural turquoise has stability problems. If it is not from Iran and it is not treated, it may turn green, white or occasionally brown within a year after it is mined. Porous material can crack or crumble. This is why almost all of the turquoise sold today has been treated—usually with a plastic substance designed to prevent discoloration and increase durability. A colorant may be added to improve the color. Sometimes turquoise is impregnated with wax to deepen the color and decrease porosity. However, the wax can pick up dirt and gradually discolor. When buying turquoise, assume it has been treated unless you are dealing with a knowledgeable, trustworthy seller who writes on the receipt "untreated natural turquoise."

The most highly valued turquoise is untreated and dense and has an even, intense sky-blue color. Usually, this type of material is from Iran. The value is reduced if the color is green or pale or if inclusions or lines called "spider-webbing" are present. Some people, though, prefer greenish colors and patterned turquoise. Prices can range from $1 a stone to a few hundred dollars for a top-quality, untreated cabochon. In the 1970's, the same cab might have sold for $2000. Turquoise in real Indian jewelry or antique pieces may be worth a lot more than loose stones of the same quality.

Fig. Tq.1 Chinese turquoise beads and a carving of untreated turquoise from the Sleeping Beauty Mine in Globe, Arizona. This mine is noted for producing high-quality turquoise.

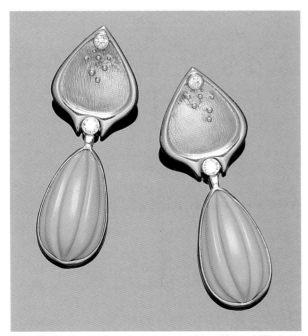

Fig. Tq.2 Turquoise earrings created by Richard Kimball. *Photo by Steve Ramsey.*

Fig. Tq.3 Turquoise bracelet purchased from Indians in Arizona. The inscription "Navaho by John Silversmith" is found on the back.

Zircon ZrSiO$_4$—Zirconium silicate
December birthstone

Zircon is not the same as cubic zirconia (CZ). Zircon is a natural gemstone with exceptional brilliance and a diamond-like luster. Cubic zirconia is a synthetic stone with a different chemical composition. When colorless and well-cut, both stones resemble diamonds. Before CZ was introduced to the market in 1976, heat-treated, colorless zircon was widely used as a diamond imitation. As a result, many people mistakenly think zircon is just a fake stone.

Zircon comes in almost every color of the spectrum. Today, most zircon sold in jewelry stores is blue. This color results from heating brownish zircon. Before the 1900's, orange or reddish-brown zircon, called **hyacinth**, was the most common type. The name "zircon" may have originated from the Persian word *zargun* meaning gold-color. Three of the main sources of zircon are Cambodia, Thailand and Sri Lanka. It is also found in Vietnam, Myanmar, Tanzania, France and Australia. Bangkok is the world's cutting and marketing center for zircon.

There is a wide variation of properties among zircons so mineralogists classify them into at least two types: those with low properties and those with high ones (RI above ≈1.90, specific gravity above ≈4.6, and a hardness of ≈7 1/2). Some zircons may be classified as an intermediate type. Zircon property ranges are given below:

RI: 1.78–2.01	SG: 3.9–4.8	Hardness: 6–6.5	Crystal System: Tetragonal
Cleavage: Imperfect and negligible		Optic Character: DR, Uniaxial positive	
Toughness: Untreated stones—fair to good; heated stones—poor to fair, chip and abrade easily			
Pleochroism: Weak to moderate except in blue stones, where it's strong blue and brownish yellow to colorless.			
Stability to Light: Some heat-treated stones may revert to their original color.			
Care Tips: Ultrasonics are risky. Avoid strong light and heat; it can cause some stones to change color.			
Treatments: Blue & colorless—routinely heated; red—commonly heated; yellow & orange—sometimes heated			

Varieties

BLUE ZIRCON: It often resembles aquamarine and blue topaz but has more fire and brilliance. The blue zircon sold in jewelry stores is heat treated and susceptible to abrasions, especially when mounted in rings. Retail prices can range from $20 to $500 per carat.

GREEN ZIRCON: Found mostly in Sri Lanka, this zircon is often grayish or yellowish. It's not uncommon for street vendors to sell it as green tourmaline or green sapphire. A curious property of green zircon is that it usually emits some level of natural radioactivity.

YELLOW, ORANGE & BROWN-RED ZIRCON: In their natural state, these zircons tend to be either brownish or pale. Heat treatment can intensify the color and reduce brown tints. To verify the colors are stable, dealers sometimes expose them for several days to the sun. Retail prices range from about $15 to $200 per carat, depending on size and quality.

COLORLESS ZIRCON: This variety occurs rarely in nature, but can be produced by heating brownish zircon. Today, CZ has replaced colorless zircon as the most popular diamond imitation.

Fig. Z.1 Zircon rings by Nanz Aalund. *Gems from Cynthia Renée Co.; photo by Robert Weldon.*

Fig. Z.2 Blue zircon earrings from Timeless Gem Designs

Center right: **Fig. Z.3** Three different colored zircons from Overland Gems

Bottom right: **Fig. Z.4** Unheated zircon from Cynthia Renée Co. *Photo by Robert Weldon.*

Ammolite pin by Fred & Kate Pearce. *Photo by Ralph Gabriner.*

Malachite & ammonite, the fossilized shellfish that is the source of ammolite. *Earrings and photo from Eve Alfillé.*

Ammolite A form of aragonite (CaCO₃) from fossilized ammonite, an extinct shellfish

Despite its ancient origins, ammolite, a multicolored gemstone, is a relative newcomer to the gem market. First sold as a gem material in 1962, it wasn't until 1983 that major production began. Some Feng Shui masters believe that ammolite has absorbed cosmic energy from the universe, which in turn is circulated back through the stone, generating health, wealth and enlightenment.

Originally discovered by the Blackfoot Indians, ammolite is mined only in Southern Alberta, Canada. Most ammolite is assembled into doublets or triplets to increase durability because solid ammolite is usually thin and fragile, If it's untreated and solid, ammolite is usually priced per carat and shaped as a freeform to maximize weight. Natural untreated ammolite retails for around $10 to $100 *per carat* depending on the quality and size. Triplets are sold by the piece and can range in retail price from $20 to $2000 *per piece* depending on quality and size. Solid treated ammolite is also priced by the piece.

Ammolite pin by Fred & Kate Pearce. *Photo by Kate Pearce.*

Extra fine quality ammolites display three or more sharp, brilliant colors with no obvious dark areas except for fine lines which separate the patches of color. The narrower the lines the better. The most prized stones are those that exhibit the full color spectrum including blue and purple, which are the rarest colors. One top quality natural ammolite piece *wholesaled* for $8000. It was 10 x 8 cm and weighed approximately 250 carats.

Red and brown are the most common colors so stones with those predominant colors sell for less. Thick dividing lines and dull, grayish colors also lower the price. Chapter 4 has additional information and photos on evaluating ammolite. For a much more in-depth discussion of ammolite, consult the Spring 2001 edition of *Gems & Gemmology.*

RI: 1.525–1.67	SG: 2.75–2.84	Hardness: 3.5–4	Reaction to chemicals: Attacked by acids
Stability to light: Stable		**Stability to heat:** breaks down and loses iridescence; avoid heat	

Toughness: Red ammolite is relatively tough, but blue and purple are brittle. Triplets with quartz or synthetic spinel tops are more durable.

Care Tips; Avoid ultrasonics, rough wear, heat and chemicals. Wipe with soft cloth & cool soapy water.

Treatments: Much of it is impregnated with an epoxy type substance to increase durability. It's *not* heat treated or irradiated. Untreated ammolite usually sells for more than treated pieces of the same quality.

Andalusite pendant by Peter Barr. *Photo by Jo Barr.*

Apatite. *Pendant & photo from Proprioro.*

Andalusite Al_2SiO_5—aluminum silicate (pronounced an′ dl oo′ site)

Andalusite is sometimes called "poor man's alexandrite" because it may appear green, red and yellow when viewed from different directions. (In technical terms, it has strong pleochroism.) Its face-up color is typically a brownish or yellowish green to orangey brown.

Andalusite was named after the Spanish province of Andalusia, where it was first found. Today its primary sources are Brazil and Sri Lanka. Fine, transparent stones above 3 carats can retail for as much as $400 per carat. Transparent commercial quality stones from 1 to 3 carats may range from $10–$75 per carat.

RI: 1.63–1.64	SG: 3.13–3.20	Hardness: 6.5–7.5	Reaction to heat: stable
Stability to light: stable		Reaction to chemicals: none	Toughness: fair to good
Care Tips: Ultrasonic cleaning is usually safe for andalusites with good clarity.			
Treatments: Usually none. Heating produces a pink color from some green stones but is rarely done.			

Apatite $Ca_5(PO_4)_3$ (F, OH, Cl)$_3$, (A mineral group)

Apatite occurs in many shades of yellow, green, blue, pink, purple, violet, and colorless as well as in cat's-eye form. It has become popular because some of the blue and green colors resemble those of the highly prized Paraiba tourmaline. Blue to green transparent apatite retails from about $25–$400 per carat depending on quality and size. Yellow apatite is more common and costs less. See figure 2.19, page 24 for another photo example of apatite .

RI: 1.63–1.65	SG: 3.16–3.23	Hardness: 5	Treatments: none known
Stability to light: usually stable, some pink may fade		Toughness: fair	
Reaction to chemicals: attacked by sulfuric & HCl acids		Reaction to heat: Loses or changes color	
Care Tips: Ultrasonics are risky. Avoid acids, high heat & rough wear; wash with warm soapy water.			

Azurite $Cu_3(CO_3)_2(OH)_2$—Copper carbonate hydroxide (pronounced azh´er rite´)

Azurite has an attractive dark blue to violet color and is found in or near copper deposits. It's often color-banded and may be found together with malachite, chrysocolla or apatite. Special care is required because azurite is soft (3.5–4 on the Mohs scale) and sensitive to heat and acids; avoid ultrasonics and chemicals. Wax or epoxy impregnation is sometimes done to increase durability, but the color is natural.

Azurite/chrysocolla & rhodochrosite. *Pin & photo from Eve Alfillé.*

Azurite and apatite. *Pendant & photo from Pearce Design.*

Benitoite $BaTiSi_3O_9$—barium titanium silicate (pronounced ben nee´toe-ite´)

Benitoite is a popular item among gem collectors because of its rarity, high brilliance, diamond-like fire and appealing natural blue color. It was named after San Benito County, California where it was discovered in 1906. Since gem-quality benitoite is mined only in that state, it was selected as the Official State Gemstone of California in October of 1985.

Benitoites over two carats are rare and can retail for as much as $6000 per carat, if you're able to find them. One- to two-carat stones may range from $800–$4000 depending on size and quality. For benitoites under one carat, retail prices are about $200–$1000 per carat. The availability of benitoite increased in 2002; nevertheless, don't expect to find it in your local jewelry store.

RI: 1.757–1.804	SG: 3.64–3.68	Hardness: 6–6.5	Toughness: fair
Pleochrism: strong blue/colorless dichroism		Optic Character: DR, uniaxial positive	
Stability to light: stable		Treatments: not treated; the color is natural	
Reaction to chemicals: attacked by hydrofluoric acid and concentrated hydrochloric acid			
Care Tips: Ultrasonics are risky. Avoid acids & rapid temperature changes. Clean in warm, soapy water			

Benitoite—State gem of California. *Photo by Robert Weldon.*

Calcite CaCO₃—Calcium carbonate

Common worldwide, calcite is the main component of marble. Mexico, Russia, Canada, Iceland, and the US are sources of transparent yellow and colorless calcite, Spain and Zaire are the sources of a pink to purple calcite variety called **cobaltocalcite**. Other colors include red, orange, green and blue. Calcite is soft (3 on the Mohs scale) and breaks easily when hit. Avoid rough wear, chemicals and heat.

Charoite A rock composed of charoite and other minerals

Charoite is a lovely stone with variegated purple, lavender and white patterns and sometimes crystals of orange, gray and black. It was discovered in 1976 during extension work on the Trans-Siberian Railroad in the Charo River area of Russia; hence the name. Typically used for carvings, charoite is also fashioned into beads and cabochons. Clean with warm soapy water, but never in an ultrasonic because the vibrations can cause it to break. It has a Mohs hardness of 5–6.

Charoite necklace by Tom DeGasperis. *Photo by Shelly Smith.*

Cobaltocalcite drusy, opal and tourmaline. *Pendant by Gary Dulac; photo by Azad.*

Diopside   CaMgSi$_2$O$_6$ — Calcium magnesium silicate (pronounced dye op' side)

The best known diopside variety is **chrome diopside**, which is deep green and found mainly in Russia and Kenya. A black star diopside is mined in India and usually has four rays, but may have six. Other diopsides may be colorless, pale green, brown and in rare cases blue or violet.

Retail prices for transparent chrome diopside typically range from about $30–$200.depending on size and quality. Wear diopside for earrings, pins and pendants, instead of rings, and clean with warm soapy water. Ultrasonics are risky.

RI: 1.66–1.72	SG: 3.22–3.38	Hardness: 5.5–6.5	Toughness: poor
Stability to light: stable		**Reaction to chemicals:** attacked by hydrofluoric acid	
Treatments: None known		**Reaction to heat:** melts under a jeweler's torch	

Fluorite   (formerly called fluorspar) CaF$_2$ — Calcium fluoride

The name "fluorite" comes from the Latin *fluere,* which means "to flow," since it melts easily and is used as a flux in the smelting of metals. The word "fluorescence" was in turn derived from fluorite because it was one of the first fluorescent minerals ever observed.

Natural and synthetic fluorite occur in a wide range of colors, including purple, pink, yellow, green and blue. It may also be multicolored or display a color change. Fluorite is popular because of its diversity, affordability and its supposed metaphysical properties as an aid to objectivity, balance and concentration.

Fluorite is the standard reference point for the hardness measure of 4 on the Mohs scale. Because of its softness and tendency to cleave (split), fluorite is principally used in carvings, but fluorite beads, pendants and earrings are also available. Avoid ultrasonics, chemicals and high heat.

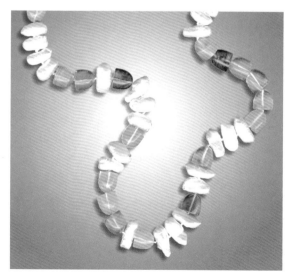

Left: Fluorite bullet-shaped beads and cultured Chinese freshwater pearl necklace.

Below: Chrome diopside earrings.

All Jewelry created by Eve Alfillé; Both photos by Matthew Arden

Rainbow obsidian from Tom DeGasperis. *Photo by Shelly Smith.*

Hematite below a fire opal. *Pin/pendant from Paula Crevoshay; photo by Azad.*

Hematite F_2O_3 — Iron oxide

Hematite has a metallic luster and is typically opaque with a dark gray to black color. When scratched or scraped it produces a characteristic reddish powder, which was used as a pigment for Egyptian cave paintings, American Indian face paint and American barns. The name "hematite" is derived from the Greek *hema* (blood) since the color of the stone's powder (streak) resembled dried blood. Major deposits are in Brazil, Canada, Venezuela and the United States.

Rainbow hematite from Eve Alfillé. *Photo by Matthew Arden.*

One variety that has become popular with designers is **rainbow hematite** from Minas Gerais, Brazil. It has an attractive iridescence resulting from a thin film of aluminum phosphate on its surface.

Because of its high density (5.12–5.78), hematite is heavy for earrings. Its hardness is 5.5–6.5 on the Mohs scale. Hematite dissolves in hydrochloric acid, but can be safely cleaned in ultrasonics. You can find it for sale at costume-jewelry prices in the form of beads, pendants, cameos and carvings.

Natural Glass Mainly SiO_2 — silicon dioxide (e.g., obsidian and moldavite)

Obsidian is a natural glass that forms when very siliceous lava with low water content cools very quickly. Most of the material used in jewelry is from North America. Obsidian usually has a black, brown or gray body color. It may be banded, exhibit a golden or silver sheen, or have white snowflake-like patterns. **Rainbow obsidian** is an iridescent, untreated variety found in Mexico and Oregon; jewelry designers like to use it to add interest to their pieces.

Natural glasses that are formed from the impact of meteorites are called **tektites**. They're named after the locality in which they're found. **Moldavite**, the best known tektite, is from the Moldau River area of Czechoslovakia and is typically yellowish to brownish green and often transparent.

Ultrasonic cleaning is usually safe for natural glass, but avoid high heat, sudden temperature changes and rough wear. The Mohs hardness is 5–6. Most material is sold at costume-jewelry prices.

Larimar from Tom DeGasperis. *Photo Shelly Smith.*

Rhodonite from Eve Alfillé. *Photo Matthew Arden.*

Larimar (Pectolite species) $NaCa_2Si_3O_8(OH)$

If you ever go on a Caribbean cruise, you'll probably see larimar jewelry for sale. Larimar is a variety of pectolite found in the Dominican Republic. It has a blue to bluish-green color, often mottled with white, and its transparency ranges from semitransparent to opaque. Attractive larimar stones are available for less than $100.

The name was given to the stone by a Dominican, Miguel Méndez, combining his daughter's name LARIssa and MAR, the Spanish word for sea. Larimar is used by some people as a healing stone associated to the thymus and thyroid glands. It is supposed to help regulate the immune system and increase speech and communication skills.

Larimar

The color of larimar is natural and not the result of treatment. It should be cleaned with warm, soapy water. Avoid ultrasonics, acids and the heat of a jeweler's torch. Larimar has an RI of about 1.50, and SG of 2.74–2.88 and a hardness of 4.5–5.

Prehnite: $Ca_2Al_2Si_3O_{10}(OH)_2$+Fe — Calcium aluminum silicate

Prehnite is found in North America, Europe, South Africa and Australia. Its color ranges from yellow to green to gray or colorless. Prehnite is typically translucent to near transparent and can occur in cat's eye form. Clean in warm soapy water. Prehnite has a Mohs hardness of 6–6.5, an RI of 1.61–1.67, and a density of 2.85–2.95.

Prehnite from Eve Alfillé. *Photo by Bower Corwin.*

Rhodonite $MnSiO_3$ (+Ca) — Manganese silicate

Rhodonite is usually pink with veins or patches of black manganese oxide and has a translucent to opaque transparency. A few rare specimens are red and transparent. Rhodonite is found in Australia, Russia, Sweden, India, Canada, Mexico, South Africa, Tanzania, the U.S. and Japan.

Some people say rhodonite has a beneficial effect upon the growth of bones and the auditory system. It's usually safe to clean it ultrasonically, but keep it away from the high heat of a jeweler's torch and acids. Rhodonite is normally not treated. It has a Mohs hardness of 5.5–5.7, an RI of 1.73–1,75 and an SG of 3.4–3.7.

Rhodochrosite and lapis brooch by Eve Alfillé. *Photo by Matthew Arden.*

Sugilite below an amethyst & ruby from Pearce Design. *Photo by Ralph Gabriner.*

Rhodochrosite $MnCO_3$—Manganese carbonate (pronounced row' duh crow'site)

The world's finest rhodochrosite is transparent, faceted and red and comes from the Sweet Home Mine in Alma, Colorado. It's rare and can retail for as much as $150–$300 per carat in weights above a carat. When it's more than 10 carats, that price can be upwards of $500 per carat. Solid red translucent stones cut as cabochons may retail for about $5–$20 per carat. Rhodochrosite became the Official State Mineral of Colorado in June 2002.

Argentina is the main source of pink banded rhodochrosite, which is semi-opaque to opaque. It's inexpensive and sold by the piece. Much of it is used for carvings, spheres and other ornamental items. Some rhodochrosite is also found in Peru, South Africa, Mexico and Japan. None of these localities are producing commercial quantities of gem faceted material; however, transparent stones from South

Rhodochrosite from Iteco, Inc. *Photo by Jeff Scovil.*

Africa are still available today, even though no major finds have occurred since the 1980's. This red to orangey-brown material typically retails from $100–$200 per carat.

Rhodochrosite is stable to light and of natural color and has a Mohs hardness of 3.5–4.5; an SG of 3.45–3.70; and an RI of 1.60–1.82. It should be cleaned in cool soapy water. Avoid ultrasonics, rough handling, heat and chemicals. Rhodochrosite is a beautiful stone for pendants, pins and earrings, but does not withstand wear in rings.

Sugilite $Na_3KLi_2(FeMnAl)_2[Si_{12}O_{30}]$ Material called sugilite is usually a combination of sugilite and other minerals such as quartz

Sugilite has a lavender to purple color. The more intense and evenly distributed the purple, and the more transparent the material, the more prized the stone. Normally, sugilite is nearly opaque but it can be semitransparent. It typically retails from about $3–$20 per carat, but semi-transparent material can sell for a lot more.

Sugilite was discovered in Southwest Japan in 1944 by Ken-ichi Sugi, for whom it was later named. In the late 1970's, sugilite from South Africa appeared on the jewelry market in the form of cabochons and beads. Today you'll find it at gem shows and in designer jewelry. It's priced both by the piece and by carat weight.

Clean sugilite with warm soapy water. Ultrasonics can be risky. Sugilite is normally not treated and has a Mohs hardness of 5.5–6.5, an SG of 2.74–2.80, and an RI of 1.60–1.61.

Sphene (Titanite) CaTiSiO$_5$ —
Calcium titanium silicate (pronounced sfeen)

Sphene is usually yellow, green, orange or brown and is noted for its diamond-like luster and exceptional fire (dispersion). It's transparent to translucent and is typically faceted. Brazil and Madagascar are the main sources, but sphene is also found in Sri Lanka, India, Austria, Canada and Switzerland.

Sphene & photo from Extrême Gioielli

RI: 1.85–2.11	SG: 3.45–3.55	Hardness: 5–5.5	Toughness: fair to poor
Stability to light: stable	Treatments: none known	Reaction to chemicals: attacked by acids	
Care Tips: Clean in warm soapy water. Avoid acids, rough wear and sudden temperature changes.			

Variscite AlPO$_4$.2H$_2$O—hydrous aluminum phosphate

Variscite resembles turquoise and has a similar pricing. The main source of variscite is Utah, but some is also found in Nevada and in the Voightland district of Germany (formerly called Variscia after which it is named).

RI: 1.56–1.59	SG: 2.4–2.6	Hardness: 3.5–5	Reaction to heat: sensitive
Stability to light: stable	Treatments: none known	Reaction to chemicals: attacked by acids	
Care Tips: Clean in warm soapy water. Avoid ultrasonics, heat and acids.			

Variscite jewelry by Tom DeGasperis. *Photo by Shelly Smith.*

Variscite and pink tourmaline slice brooch by Eve Alfillé. *Photo by Matthew Arden.*

Test Your Gem IQ

In most cases you can't identify a gem just by looking at it, but you can make good guesses. Try to identify the gems in these designer pieces. The answers are at the bottom of the page.

Fig. 1 Gary Dulac. *Photo: John Parrish.*

Fig. 2 Pearce Design. *Photo: Kate Pearce.*

Fig. 3 Eve Alfillé. *Photo by Bower Corwin.*

Fig. 4 Eve Alfillé. *Photo by Matthew Arden.*

Fig. 1 From top: 0.50 ct tsavorite, 6.18 ct blue chalcedony, boulder opal, 30.05 ct sugilite
Fig. 2 From top: peridot beads, peridot trilliant, tourmaline, chrysocolla quartz
Fig. 3 From top: gem chrysocolla, bloodstone, Montana agate; turquoise, variscite and prehnite
Fig. 4 Wings: sapphires, emeralds, boulder opals and diamonds; eyes: emeralds; head & thorax: moonstones; body: a suite of faceted rainbow labradorite in graduated hues

12

Caring for your Gems

C ars, furniture and clothing will look better and last longer if you take care of them. The same is true of gems. Clothing manufacturers sew written instructions into their products. They'll say, for example, "dry clean only," "no bleach," "cool iron," etc. It's not possible to place this kind of information on gems. Therefore, you must rely on salespeople, brochures and books for instructions on how to look after your gem and jewelry purchases.

It's important to realize that colored gemstones are not as durable as diamonds. Diamonds are used as drills, they're boiled in acid, they're heated and then plunged in water. Don't treat colored gems in this manner. Many gems are very susceptible to **thermal shock**—sudden temperature changes. These include emerald, garnet, kunzite, opal, peridot, quartz, tanzanite, topaz and tourmaline. You should not, for example, lay in the sun and then jump in a swimming pool while wearing these gems, nor should you go from a hot oven to a cold sink of water or from a hot tub to a cold shower. If you do, the sudden temperature change could possibly cause the stones to crack or shatter.

With some stones, you should avoid heat in general. These include amethyst, emerald, kunzite, malachite, opal, red tourmaline and turquoise. Don't leave these gems sitting on a sunny window sill or wear them to the beach. The heat might make amethyst, kunzite and red tourmaline fade and it could dry out and discolor the fillings in emerald. It could cause small cracks in some malachite, opal and turquoise.

Malachite and turquoise are unusually sensitive to chemicals. Ammonia and acid solutions as well as everyday products such as perfumes and lotions can harm them. Pickling solutions used by jewelers and some acids will etch the surface of peridot. Solvents such as alcohol and acetone will gradually dissolve the fillers in emeralds and other oiled or filled stones. Dyed lapis, dyed jade and other dyed stones are also adversely affected by solvents. Chlorine can gradually pit and dissolve gold alloys. The pitting can also occur while swimming or while soaking in a hot tub with chlorine.

The safest way to clean a gemstone is to wash it in lukewarm water using a mild liquid soap or detergent that contains no ammonia. Then dry it with a soft, lint-free cloth. If the dirt can't be washed off with a cloth, try using a toothpick or a Water Pik to remove it. If that doesn't work, have it professionally cleaned. Jewelers often clean stones with ultrasonic cleaners, which send high frequency sound waves through solutions. The vibrating fluid removes built-up dirt, but it can also shake poorly-set stones from their mountings and damage some types of gems. The table on the next page indicates which stones should not be cleaned in ultrasonics. Most of the data in the chart is from the GIA *Gem Reference Guide*, an article by Deborah Martin in the summer 1987 issue of *Gems and Gemology* entitled "Gemstone Durability: Design to Display," and an article by Howard Rubin entitled "Jewelers' Guide to Gemstone Handling."

Gemstone	Ultrasonic, safe?	Comments
Aquamarine	Use caution	
Chalcedony	Use caution	Chemicals may attack dyed stones
Chrysoberyl	Usually safe	
Diamond	Usually safe	Ammonia, acids and repeated ultrasonic cleaning may damage some fracture fillings
Emerald	Avoid	Avoid heat and solvents like acetone and alcohol
Garnet	Use caution	Avoid thermal shock; ultrasonics are risky if liquid inclusions are present
Iolite	Risky	Avoid acids and thermal shock
Jade	Usually safe	Acids can affect polish on stones. Avoid solvents and ultrasonics if dyed.
Kunzite	Avoid	Avoid heat and strong light to prevent fading
Lapis Lazuli	Avoid	Avoid acids, acetone and other solvents
Malachite	Avoid	Avoid chemicals and heat
Moonstone	Avoid	Avoid heat
Opal	Avoid	Avoid thermal shock
Peridot	Use caution	Avoid acids and pickling solutions
Quartz	Use caution	Avoid thermal shock
Transparent Ruby & Sapphire	Use caution	
Star Ruby & Sapphire	Risky	Avoid ultrasonics with black star sapphires and with oiled or dyed stones
Spinel	Usually safe	
Tanzanite	Avoid	Avoid thermal shock
Topaz	Avoid	Avoid thermal shock
Tourmaline	Risky	Avoid thermal shock
Turquoise	Avoid	Avoid heat and chemicals
Zircon	Risky	Avoid thermal shock

Ultrasonic cleaners should also be avoided with:

♦ Badly flawed stones of any species—they can be further damaged by ultrasonic cleaning.

♦ Oiled and/or dyed stones—the oil and dye may be removed, often quickly.

♦ Stones with glass-filled cavities—the filling may fall out.

♦ Any kind of fracture-filled stone, including diamond. The cleaning solution or vibration could cause the fillings to gradually cloud, discolor or be removed.

You may be wondering why the preceding table says to use caution when cleaning certain gems in ultrasonic cleaners. These gems are sometimes likely to have inclusions that weaken the stone, but it's usually safe to clean them ultrasonically.

Some stones are more susceptible to knocks and bumps than others. This is because of their easy cleavage (ability to split along certain crystal planes). Kunzite, tanzanite, iolite, topaz and feldspars such as moonstone and sunstone all fit in this category. If these gems are knocked lightly just right at a specific angle against a wall or furniture, they can sometimes crack. Diamonds also cleave, but it normally takes a hard blow or lots of pressure to create diamond cleavage. So don't assume that a tanzanite or a topaz can withstand the same abuse as a diamond. You must treat them with much more care.

The most durable colored stones are jade, ruby, sapphire, chrysoberyl and spinel. Jade is softer than many gems, but its toughness (resistance to chipping, breaking and cracking) surpasses all other gem materials, including diamond. The other stones listed in the table can also provide good wear. Just treat them as you would a fine silk scarf or any other accessory.

Storing Your Jewelry

When you store jewelry, protection from theft and damage should be a prime consideration. A jewelry box can protect pieces from damage if they are stored individually, but it is one of the first places burglars look when they break into a home. So it's best to reserve jewelry boxes for costume jewelry when they are displayed on tables or dressers.

Jewelry pieces should be wrapped separately in soft material or placed individually in pouches or the pockets of padded jewelry bags. If a piece is placed next to or on top of other jewelry, the metal mountings or the stones can get scratched. Use your imagination to find a secure place in your house to hide jewelry pouches, bags and boxes. If expensive jewelry is seldom worn, it's best to keep it in a safe deposit box.

Miscellaneous Tips

♦ Avoid wearing jewelry (especially rings) while participating in contact sports or doing housework, gardening, repairs, etc. In fact, it's a good idea to take most colored-stone jewelry off when you come home and change into casual clothes. If during rough work you want to wear a ring for sentimental reasons or to avoid losing it, wear protective gloves. However, even gloves won't offer full protection.

♦ Occasionally check your jewelry for loose stones. Shake it or tap it lightly with your forefinger while holding it next to your ear. If you hear the stones rattle or click, have a jeweler tighten the prongs.

♦ Don't remove rings by pulling on any of their gemstones. Instead grasp the metal ring portion. This will help prevent the stones from coming loose and getting dirty.

♦ When you set jewelry near a sink, make sure the drains are plugged or that the piece is put in a protective container or on a spindle. Otherwise, don't take the jewelry off.

♦ Take a photo of your jewelry (a macro lens is helpful). Just lay it all together on a table for the photo. If the jewelry is ever lost or stolen, you'll have documentation to help you remember and prove what you had.

♦ Clean your jewelry on a regular basis. Once a week is not too often for a ring that is worn daily. Risky cleaning procedures can be avoided by regular cleaning.

♦ About every six months, have a jewelry professional check your ring for loose stones or wear on the mounting. Many stores will do this free of charge, and they'll be happy to answer your questions regarding gem care. Jewelers want you to enjoy the jewelry you purchase from them. You will. Just treasure it and take good care of it.

Birthstones & Anniversary Stones

Birthstones established in 1912 by the American
National Retail Jewelers' Association:

January	Garnet	July	Ruby
February	Amethyst	August	Peridot or sardonyx
March	Aquamarine or bloodstone	September	Sapphire
April	Diamond	October	Opal or tourmaline
May	Emerald	November	Topaz
June	Pearl or moonstone	December	Turquoise or lapis lazuli

Anniversary Stones

1. Gold
2. Garnet
3. Pearl
4. Blue topaz
5. Sapphire
6. Amethyst
7. Onyx
8. Tourmaline
9. Lapis lazuli
10. Diamond
11. Turquoise

12. Jade
13. Citrine
14, Opal
15. Ruby
16. Imperial topaz & peridot
17. Amethyst
18. Garnet
19. Aquamarine
20. Emerald
23. Blue sapphire
25. Silver

26. Blue star sapphire
30. Pearl
35. Coral & Emerald
39. Cat's eye
40. Ruby
45. Alexandrite & sapphire
50. Gold
52. Star ruby
55. Alexandrite & emerald
60. Diamond

Astral Stones

Aquarius (January 22–February 21)	Garnet
Pisces (February 22–March 21)	Amethyst
Aries (Bloodstone–April 20)	Bloodstone
Taurus (April 21–May 21)	Sapphire
Gemini (May 22–June 21)	Agate
Cancer (June 22–July 22)	Emerald
Leo (July 23–August 22)	Onyx
Virgo (August 23–September 22)	Carnelian
Libra (September 23–October 23)	Peridot
Scorpio (October 24–November 21)	Aquamarine
Sagittarius (November 22–December 21)	Imperial Topaz
Capricorn (December 22–January 21)	Ruby

Suppliers of Jewelry & Stones for Photographs

Cover photo: Cynthia Renée Co., Fallbrook, CA
Inside front cover photos: Top photo: Hubert Inc., Los Angeles, CA
    Bottom photo: Gary Dulac Goldsmith, Inc., Vero Beach, FL
Inside back cover photos: Top photo: Gordon Aatlo, Norma Jewelers, San Carlos, CA
    Bottom photo: Mellika Co., Inc. (Paula Crevoshay Designer), Albuquerque, NM
Half-title page photo: Gordon Aatlo, Norma Jewelers, San Carlos, CA
Photo facing title page: Hubert Inc., Los Angeles, CA
Title page: Cynthia Renée Co., Fallbrook, CA

Chapter 1
Figs. 1.1 & 1.2 Fred Mouawad, Bangkok, Thailand
Figs. 1.3 & 1.19 Eve J. Alfillé Ltd., Evanston, IL
Fig. 1.4 Port Royal Antique Jewelry, Naples, FL
Fig. 1.5 American Gemological Laboratories, New York, NY
Fig. 1,9 and Pg 13 Cat's eye: Andrew Sarosi, Los Angeles, CA
Pg. 13 Moonstone: Timeless Gem Designs, Los Angeles, CA
Pg. 13 Ammolite: Korite International, Calgary, Canada
Pg. 13 Alexandrite: Overland Gems, Los Angeles, CA
Figs. 1.20 & 1.21 Dancing Designs Jewelry (Tom DeGasperis), Bethlehem, PA
Fig. 1.22 Gary Dulac Goldsmith, Inc., Vero Beach, FL
Fig. 1.23 Tom Harmon, Crane, Montana
Fig. 1.25 Josam Diamond Trading Corporation, Los Angeles, CA

Chapter 2
Figs. 2.1 & 2.2 Josam Diamond Trading Corporation, Los Angeles, CA
Figs. 2.3, 2.6, 2.13, 2.35, 2.44 Extrême Gioielli, Valenza (AL), Italy
Figs. 2.5 & 2.43 Fred & Kate Pearce of Pearce Design, West Lebanon, NH
Figs. 2.8, 2.9, 2.22 to 2.27 Hubert Inc., Los Angeles, CA
Fig. 2.14 Mark Schneider, Long Beach, CA
Fig. 2.15 Cynthia Renée Co., Fallbrook, CA
Fig. 2.18 David Clay Zava, David Clay Co., Fallbrook, CA
Fig. 2.19 Eve J. Alfillé Ltd., Evanston, IL
Figs. 2.28 & 2.29 Mark Gronlund Custom Jewelry Shop, Enterprise, FL
Fig. 2.30 Speira Gems, Ashland, OR
Fig. 2.31 Burdett A. Milkens Designs (BAM), Monroe, MI
Figs. 2.32 & 2.33 Timeless Gem Designs, Los Angeles, CA
Fig. 2.34 The Diamond Dove, Inc., Boulder, CO
Fig. 2.36 Gemscapes Sculptured Gemstones, Southfield, MI
Figs. 2.37, 2.42 & 2.44 Mellika Co., Inc. (Paula Crevoshay Designer), Albuquerque, NM
Fig. 2.38 William Cox Gem Carvings, Provo, UT
Figs. 2.39 & 2.40 Glenn Lehrer Designs, San Rafael, CA
Figs. 2.45 & 2.47 Gary Dulac Goldsmith, Inc., Vero Beach, FL
Figs. 2.46, 2.48, & 2.49 Dancing Designs Jewelry (Tom DeGasperis), Bethlehem, PA

Chapter 4

Fig. 4.2 Color Masters Gem Corp, New York, NY
Figs. 4.3 & 4.5 Harry Winston, Inc., New York, NY
Fig. 4.4 Carrie G., Los Angeles, CA
Fig. 4.6 Korite International, Calgary, Canada
Figs. 4.7 & 4.8 Fred & Kate Pearce of Pearce Design, West Lebanon, NH

Chapter 5

Figs. 5.1 Tom Harmon, Crane, Montana
Fig. 5.4 Jack S. D. Abraham of Precious Gem Resources, New York, NY
Figs. 5.9 & 5.10 Danny & Ronny Levy Fine Gems, Los Angeles, CA
Figs. 5.11 & 5.12 Overland Gems, Los Angeles, CA

Chapter 6

Fig. 6.2 Cynthia Renée Co., Fallbrook, CA
Figs. 6.3 & 6.4 Josam Diamond Trading Corporation, Los Angeles, CA
Fig. 6.8 Glenn Lehrer Designs, San Rafael, CA
Fig. 6.10 Mark Gronlund Custom Jewelry Shop, Enterprise, FL

Chapter 7

Fig. 7.1 Hubert Inc., Los Angeles, Ca
Figs. 7.2 to 7.4 Andrew Sarosi, Los Angeles, CA
Fig 7.5 Asian Institute of Gemological Sciences, Bangkok, Thailand
Fig. 7.7 Danny & Ronny Levy Fine Gems, Los Angeles, CA

Chapter 11

Fig. Am.1 Cynthia Renée Co., Fallbrook, CA
Fig. Am.2 Peggy Croft Wax Sculpturing, Los Angeles, CA
Figs. Am.3 & Am.10 Linda K. Quinn Designs, Strafford, MO
Fig. Am.4 Timeless Gem Designs, Los Angeles, CA
Fig. Am.5 Gordon Aatlo, Norma Jewelers, San Carlos, CA
Fig. Am 6 The Diamond Dove, Inc., Boulder, CO
Fig. Am.7 Dancing Designs Jewelry (Tom DeGasperis), Bethlehem, PA
Fig. Am 9 Extrême Gioielli, Valenza (AL), Italy
Fig. Ca.1 William Cox Gem Carvings, Provo, UT
Figs. Ca.2 & Ca.8 Richard H. Kimball Designs, Inc., Denver, CO
Figs. Ca.3 & Ca.18 Dancing Designs Jewelry (Tom DeGasperis), Bethlehem, PA
Figs. Ca.4, Ca.14–Ca.17 Fred & Kate Pearce of Pearce Design, West Lebanon, NH
Fig. Ca.9 Timeless Gem Designs, Los Angeles, CA
Fig. Ca.10 Michael Francis & Co., Phoenix, AZ
Fig. Ca.11 Murphy Design, Minneapolis, MN
Figs. Al.1 to Al.3 Andrew Sarosi, Los Angeles, CA
Fig. Al.4 Carrie G., Los Angeles, CA
Fig. Em.1 Gemscapes Sculptured Gemstones, Southfield, MI
Fig. Em.2 Color Masters Gem Corp, New York, NY
Fig. Em.3 Robert Trisko Jewelry Sculptures, Waite Park, MN
Fig. Em.4 Cynthia Renée Co., Fallbrook, CA
Fig. Em.5 Glenn Lehrer Designs, San Rafael, CA
Fig. Em.6 Harry Winston, Inc., New York, NY
Fig. Em.7 & G.7 Carrie G., Los Angeles, CA
Figs. G.1, G.5 & G.6 Cynthia Renée Co., Fallbrook, CA
Fig. G.2 Gary Dulac Goldsmith, Inc., Vero Beach, FL
Fig. G.3 Mark Schneider. Long Beach, CA
Fig. G.4 Gary Dulac Goldsmith, Inc., Vero Beach, FL
Fig. G.8 Dan Miller Jewelry, Laguna Beach, CA
Figs. G.9 and I.1 Proprioro, San Francisco, CA

Bibliography

Books and Booklets

Arem, Joel. *Color Encyclopedia of Gemstones.* New York: Chapman & Hall, 1987.

Bauer, Jaroslav & Bouska, Vladimir. *Pierres Precieuses et Pierres Fines.* Paris: Bordas, 1985.

Bauer, Dr. Max. *Precious Stones.* New York: Dover Publications, 1968.

Beesley, C. R. *Gemstone Training Manual.* American Gemological Laboratories.

Carmona, Charles. *Complete Handbook for Gemstone Weight Estimation.* Los Angeles: Gemania Publishing, 1998.

Ciprani, Curzio & Borelli, Alessandro. *Simon & Schuster's Guide to Gems and Precious Stones.* New York: Simon and Schuster, 1986.

Cody, Andrew. *Australian Precious Opal.* Melbourne: Andrew Cody Party Ltd., 1991.

Dennis, Daniel. *Gems, A Lively Guide for the Casual Collector.* New York: HarryN. Abrams, Inc. 1999.

Downing, Paul. *Opal Identification and Value.* Estes Park. Colorado: Majestic Press, 1992.

Federman, David & Hammid, Tino. *Consumer Guide to Colored Gemstones.* Shawnee Mission, KS: Modern Jeweler, 1989.

Gemological Institute of America. *Gem Reference Guide.* Santa Monica, CA: GIA, 1988.
Gemological Institute of America, *The GIA Diamond Dictionary, Third Edition.* Santa Monica, CA: GIA, 1993.

Geolat, Patti, Van Northrup, C., Federman, David. *The Professional's Guide to Jewelry Insurance Appraising.* Lincolnshire, IL: Vance Publishing Corporation, 1994.

Gump, Richard. *Jade Stone of Heaven.* Garden City, NY: Doubleday, 1962.

Gubelin, Eduard J. & Koivula, John I. *Photoatlas of Inclusions in Gemstones.* Zurich: ABC Edition, 1986.

Gubelin, Eduard & Erni, Franz-Zaver, *Gemstones, Symbols of Beauty & Power,* Tucson, AZ: Geoscience Press, 2000.

Hall, Cally. *Gemstones,* Eyewitness Handbooks. London: Dorling Kindersley, 1994.
Hall, Cally. *Gems & Precious Stones,* Edison, NJ: Chartwell Books Inc., 1998.

Hanneman, W. Wm. *Naming Gem Garnets.* Poulsbo, WA: Hanneman Gemological Instruments, 2000.

Harmon, Tom. *The River Runs North, A Story of Montana Moss Agate.* Crane, Montana: Cheryl & Tom Harmon Book Distributors, 2000.

Hoover, D B. *Topaz.* Oxford: Butterworth-Heinemann Ltd, 1992.

Hughes, Richard W. *Corundum.* London: Butterworth-Heinemann, 1990
Hughes, Richard W. *Ruby & Sapphire,* Boulder, CO: RWH Publishing, 1997.

Jewelers of America. *The Gemstone Enhancement Manual.* New York: Jewelers of America, 1990-94.

Jewell, Bill. *The Buying Guide to Black Opals.* North South Wales: Mineral Resources, 1996.

Keller, Peter. *Gemstones of East Africa.* Phoenix: Geoscience Press Inc., 1992.

Kraus, Edward H. & Slawson, Chester B. *Gems & Gem Minerals.* New York: McGraw-Hill, 1947.

Kunz, George Frederick. *The Curious Lore of Precious Stones.* New York: Bell, 1989.
Kunz, George Frederick. *Gems & Precious Stones of North America.* New York: Dover, 1968.

Liddicoat, Richard T. *Handbook of Gem Identification*. Santa Monica, CA: GIA, 1993

Marcum, David. *Fine Gems and Jewelry*. Homewood, IL: Dow Jones-Irwin, 1986.

Matlins, Antoinette L. & Bonanno, A. *Jewelry & Gems: The Buying Guide*. South Woodstock, VT: Gemstone Press, 1993.

Miller, Anna M. *Gems and Jewelry Appraising*. New York: Van Nostrand Reinhold Company, 1988.

Mumme, I. A. *The Emerald*. Port Hacking, N.S.W.: Mumme Publications, 1982.

Nassau, Kurt. *Gems Made by Man*. Santa Monica, CA: Gemological Institute of America, 1980.

Nassau, Kurt. *Gemstone Enhancement, Second Edition*. London: Butterworths, 1994.

Newman, Renée. *Diamond Ring Buying Guide, 6th Edition*. Los Angeles: Intl. Jewelry Publications, 2002.

Newman, Renee. *Gem & Jewelry Pocket Guide,*. Los Angeles: Intl. Jewelry Publications, 2001.

Newman, Renée. *Ruby, Sapphire, & Emerald Buying Guide, 2nd Edition*. Los Angeles: Intl. Jewelry Publications, 2002.

O'Donoghue, Michael. *Identifying Man-made Gems*. London: N.A.G. Press, 1983.

O'Donoghue, Michael. *Synthetic, Imitation & Treated Gemstones*, Oxford, Butterworth-Heinemann, 1997.

O'Leary, Barrie. *A Field Guide to Australian Opals*. E. Malvern, Australia: Gemcraft Publications, 1984.

Pough, Frederick. *Rocks & Minerals*. Boston: Houghton Mifflin, 1983.

Ramsey, John L. & Ramsey, Laura J. *The Gem Collector's Handbook*. Seattle: Boa Vista Press, 1995.

Read, Peter G. *Gemmology*. Butterworth Heinemann, 1991,

Rouse, John D. *Garnet*. London: Butterworths, 1986.

Rubin, Howard. *Grading & Pricing with GemDialogue*. New York: GemDialogue Marketing Co., 1986.

Schumann, Walter. *Gemstones of the World*. New York: Sterling, 1997.

Schwartz, Dietmar. *Esmeraldas, Inclusoes em Gemas*. Ouro Preto, Brazil. Federal University of Ouro Preto, 1987.

Sinkankas, John. *Emerald and other Beryls*. Prescott, AZ: Geoscience Press, 1989.

Sinkankas, John. *Gemstone & Mineral Data Book*. Prescott, Arizona: Geoscience Press, 1988.

Sinkankas, John and Read, Peter. *Beryl*. London: Butterworths. 1986.

Sevdermish, M. & Mashiah, A. *The Dealer's Book of Gems and Diamonds*. Israel: Mada Avanim Yekarot Ltd., 1996.

Sofianides, Anna & Harlow, George. *Gems & Crystals from the American Museum of Natural History*. New York: Simon & Schuster, 1990.

Suwa, Yasukazu. *Gemstones Quality & Value* (English Edition). Gemological Institute of America and Suwa & Son, Inc., 1994.

Suwa, Yasukazu. *Gemstones Quality & Value: Volume 2*. Tokyo: Sekai Bunka Publishing, Inc., 1997.

Walters, Raymond. *The Power of Gemstones*. Chartwell Books, 1996.

Webster, Robert. *Gems, Fourth Edition*. London: Butterworths, 1983.

White, John S. *The Smithsonian Treasury Minerals and Gems*. Washington D.C.: Smithsonian Institution Press, 1991.

Woodward, Christine & Harding, Roger. *Gemstones*. New York: Sterling Publishing Co. 1988.

Wykoff, Gerald L. *Beyond the Glitter*. Washington DC: Adamas, 1982.

Zucker, Benjamin. *How to Buy & Sell Gems: Everyone's Guide to Rubies, Sapphires, Emeralds & Diamonds*. New York: Times Books, 1979.

Periodicals

Auction Market Resource for Gems & Jewelry. P. O. Box 7683 Rego Park, NY. 11374.

Australian Gemmologist. Brisbane: Gemmological Association of Australia

Canadian Gemmologist. Toronto: Canadian Gemmological Association.

Colored Stone. Devon, PA: *Lapidary Journal* Inc.

GAA Market Monitor Precious Gem Appraisal/Buying Guide. Pittsburgh, PA: GAA.

Gem. Radnor, PA: Chilton Publishing Co.

Gems and Gemology. Santa Monica, CA: Gemological Institute of America.

Gem & Jewellery News. London. Gemmological Association and Gem Testing Laboratory of Great Britain.

Gemstone Price Reports. Brussels: Ubige S.P.R.L.

The Guide. 650 Dundee Rd. Suite 465, Northbrook, IL: Gemworld International, Inc.

Lapidary Journal. Devon, PA: *Lapidary Journal* Inc.

JewelSiam. Bangkok, Thailand.

Jewelers Circular Keystone. Radnor, PA: Chilton Publishing Co.

Jewelers' Quarterly Magazine. Sonoma, CA.

Journal of Gemmology, London: Gemmological Association and Gem Testing Laboratory of Great Britain.

Michelsen Gemstone Index. Pompano Beach, FL: Gem Spectrum.

Modern Jeweler. Lincolnshire, IL: Vance Publishing Inc.

National Jeweler. New York: Gralla Publications.

Palmieri's GAA Market Monitor. Pittsburgh, PA:

Professional Jeweler. Philadelphia: Bond Communications.

Rock & Gem. Ventura, CA: Miller Magazines, Inc.

Miscellaneous: Courses, notes, and leaflets

Gemological Institute of America Appraisal Seminar handbook.

Gemological Institute of America Gem Identification Course.

Gemological Institute of America Colored Stone Grading Course.

Gemological Institute of America Colored Stone Grading Course Charts, 1984 & 1989.

Gemological Institute of America Colored Stones Course. 1980 & 1989 editions.

Gemological Institute of America Jewelry Sales Course.

Jewelers of America. *A Guide to What You Should Know About Colored Gemstones.*

Rubin, Howard. "The Effects of Lighting on Gemstone Colors."

Rubin, Howard. "Jewelers Guide to Gemstone Handling." Rego Park, NY: GemDialogue Systems, Inc.

Index

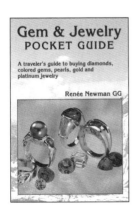

Pearl Buying Guide

How to Evaluate, Identify, Select and Care for Pearls & Pearl Jewelry

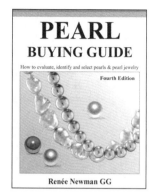

"Copious color photographs . . . explains how to appraise and distinguish among all varieties of pearls . . . takes potential buyers and collectors through the ins and outs of the pearl world."

Publisher's Weekly

"An indispensable guide to judging [pearl] characteristics, distinguishing genuine from imitation, and making wise choices . . . useful to all types of readers, from the professional jeweler to the average patron . . . **highly recommended."**

Library Journal

"A well written, beautifully illustrated book designed to help retail customers, jewelry designers, and store buyers make informed buying decisions about the various types of pearls and pearl jewelry. The photos are abundant and well chosen, and the use of a coated stock contributes to the exceptional quality of the reproduction. Consumers also will find this book a source of accurate and easy-to-understand information about a topic that has become increasingly complex."

Gems & Gemology

"If you're thinking of investing in pearls, invest $20 first in the Pearl Buying Guide. . . . Even if you already own pearls, this book has good tips on care and great ideas on ways to wear pearls."

San Jose Mercury News

156 pages, 208 color & b/w photos, 7" x 9", ISBN 0-929975-35-9, $19.95 US

Ruby, Sapphire & Emerald Buying Guide

How to Evaluate, Identify, Select & Care for these Gemstones

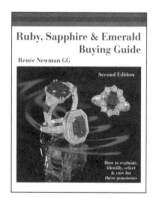

"Solid, informative and comprehensive . . . dissects each aspect of ruby and sapphire value in detail . . . a wealth of grading information . . . a definite thumbs-up. There is something here for everyone."

C. R. Beesley, President, American Gemological Laboratories.

Jewelers' Circular Keystone

"The best produced book on gemstones I have yet seen in this price range. This is the book for anyone who buys, sells or studies gemstones. This style of book (and similar ones by the same author) is the only one I know which introduces actual trade conditions and successfully combines a good deal of gemmology with them. . . . **Buy it, read it, keep it."**

Michael O'Donoghue, *Journal of Gemmology*

An up-to-date, illustrated, reliable guide on how to purchase a ruby, sapphire or emerald. Of particular value are chapters devoted to the assessment of colour and clarity, value enhancing treatments, synthetics and imitations...and the desirable features of star ruby and sapphire. . . . The accuracy and clarity of this guide's information sets a standard to be emulated. "

Australian Gemmologist

164 pages, 178 color & 21 b/w photos, 7" x 9", ISBN 0-929975-33-2, $19.95 US

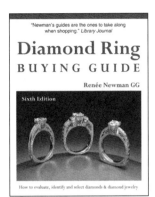

"Newman's guides are the ones to take along when shopping." *Library Journal*

Diamond Ring
BUYING GUIDE

Renée Newman GG

Sixth Edition

How to evaluate, identify and select diamonds & diamond jewelry

Diamond Ring Buying Guide
How to Evaluate, Identify, Select & Care for Diamonds & Diamond Jewelry

Includes chapters on diamond treatments, gold, platinum, setting styles, ring mountings, and diamond imitations.

"An entire course on judging diamonds in 156 pages of well-organized information . . . The photos are excellent . . . Clear and concise, it serves as a check-list for the purchase and mounting of a diamond . . . another fine update in a series of books that are useful to both the jewelry industry and consumers."

Gems & Gemology

"Priceless gem of a book . . . Warns you of scams other books ignore or gloss over. Topics covered include diamond terms, the 4C's, chart of actual sizes in carats, stunning color photos of diamond cuts and shapes, photos of diamond colors, treated diamonds. . . . Then there are photos to help you tell the difference between fake and real, fracture fills, synthetic diamonds. There are even chapters devoted to gold rings and platinum rings. Buying tips, custom ring tips, diamond cleaning, preventing diamond switching, and lots more. This truly is a diamond bible."

Jeff Ostroff, *BridalTips.com*

156 pages, 193 color & b/w photos, 7" X 9", ISBN 0-929975-32-4, $17.95 US

Gold & Platinum
Jewelry Buying Guide

How to Judge, Buy, Test & Care for It

Renée Newman

Gold & Platinum Jewelry Buying Guide
How to Judge, Buy, Test & Care for It

"Enjoyable reading . . . profusely illustrated with color photographs showing not only the beauty of finished jewelry but close-ups and magnification of details such as finish, settings, flaws and fakes . . . sophisticated enough for professionals to use . . . highly recommended . . . **Newman's guides are the ones to take along when shopping."**

Library Journal

"This book should be required reading for consumers and jewelers alike! It offers step-by-step instructions for how to examine and judge the quality of craftsmanship and materials even if you know nothing about jewelry. If you are thinking of buying, making or selling jewelry as a hobby, as a career or just one time, then this book is a great place to start."

Jeweler's Circular Keystone, Alan Revere, master goldsmith

156 pages, 127 color, 67 b/w photos, 6¾" x 9", ISBN 0-929975-29-4, $19.95 US

Available at bookstores, jewelry supply stores or by mail

Order Form

TITLE	Price Each	Quantity	Total
Gemstone Buying Guide	$19.95		
Diamond Ring Buying Guide, 6th Edition	$17.95		
Ruby, Sapphire & Emerald Buying Guide	$19.95		
Gold & Platinum Jewelry Buying Guide	$19.95		
Pearl Buying Guide	$19.95		
Diamond Handbook (available April 2005)	$18.95		
Gem & Jewelry Pocket Guide	$11.95		
Osteoporosis from a Patient's Point of View: A Consumer Approach to Strong Bones & Good Health by Newman (Available after 7/05)	$14.95		
		Book Total	
SALES TAX for California residents only		(book total x $.0825)	
SHIPPING: USA: first book $2.00, each additional copy $1.25 Foreign – surface mail: first book $6.00 ea. addl. $4.00 Canada & Mexico - airmail: first book $6.50, ea. addl. $4.00 All other foreign destinations - airmail: first book $11.00, ea. addl. $7.00			
TOTAL AMOUNT with tax (if applicable) and shipping (Pay foreign orders with an international money order or a check drawn on a U.S. bank.)		**TOTAL**	

Mail check or money order in U.S. funds

To: International Jewelry Publications
P.O. Box 13384
Los Angeles, CA 90013-0384 USA

Ship to:

Name_____

Address_____

City_____ State or Province_____

Postal or Zip Code_____ Country _____